DEDICATION

To Wilma Chestnut and Family

The Wilma Chestnut Story

By Karl Evanzz

New Wave Books

Published by New Wave Books.
Baltimore, Maryland.
Printed by: United Book Press, Baltimore

First Edition.

ISBN13: 978-0-9779112-1-9

New Wave Books and colophon are registered trademarks of New Wave Books.

Cover concept by Karl Evanzz
Book design by Karl Evanzz
Photos ©by Wilma Chestnut unless otherwise indicated.

Includes bibliographic references and index.
Printed in the United States of America

10 9 8 7 6 5 4 3 2 1

This Book
Belongs to

Also by KARL EVANZZ

The Judas Factor: The Plot to Kill Malcolm X (1992)

The Messenger: The Rise and Fall of Elijah Muhammad (1999)

I Am The Greatest: The Best Quotations from Muhammad Ali (2002)

Dancing with the Devil: How Puff Burned the Bad Boys of Hip Hp (2009)

(with Mark Curry)

CONTENTS

CONTENTS

CHAPTER 1

Nightmare

"Damn, this is the weirdest dream I've ever had."

I sat up against the sofa. It felt like I was awake but knew I couldn't be because I couldn't see anything. I squeezed my eyes shut and opened them quickly, expecting light and snapshots of the room to come into focus. Instead, there was only darkness. It was as if they weren't even open.

Since I knew I wasn't blind, I assumed that this was one of those dreams about a dream. I figured that my inability to wake up was part of a bad dream I had earlier where a man was choking me.

In the dream, I lay down on the sofa and went back to sleep.

A little while later, I was awake again.

This time I knew I wasn't dreaming. Once again, I squeezed my eyes shut and then tried to open them as wide as I could. They felt heavy and swollen. No matter how hard I tried, I could not see anything.

I scratched my arm and made a fist, and then I rubbed my leg, trying to make sure that my reactions were real. Everything felt normal.

I turned my head from side to side, listening for the slightest sound. I didn't hear the television but I could hear sounds from outside. I called the names of the children whom I was babysitting. Their responses would prove that I was awake.

I didn't hear a sound. The apartment was dead quiet.

I became more and more anxious as I ran out of ideas about how to make my eyes see something.

My head started aching so badly that I squeezed my forehead with my left hand, trying to reduce the pounding. The intense pain and my inability to see made it difficult to focus on anything for more than a few seconds.

"All right now, calm down," I said to myself as I tried to concentrate. "Just think about what you were doing before you took a nap."

I remembered putting the babies to bed for their afternoon nap. That was around two o'clock. I knew this because my favorite soap opera, NBC-TV's "Another World," had just came on. That's when someone knocked at the door.

"Ronnie!"

Ronnie Clower, my best friend's boyfriend, had stopped by with several friends. I must have fallen asleep when they were here.

For some reason, I kept getting flashbacks of the man who was choking me in the dream I had earlier. Then I recalled that Ronnie left with his friends but they had all come back.

Still, something wasn't right.

Suddenly I remembered that Ronnie's friends had come upstairs while Ronnie was downstairs to talk to some girl. I gave several glasses of water to one of them.

"Oh, my God!"

The man I gave the water to was the same man choking me in my dream. He smelled of liquor, cigarettes, and funky body odors.

I struggled for air as I fought to remove his hands from around my neck. Just when I pulled them away, the youngest visitor put his hands over my eyes and pulled me backwards, forcing me to fall.

As the events fell into place, I wondered if the boy who covered my eyes had put something in them. They didn't hurt, but they felt so swollen that it scared me. It took me several minutes to muster the courage to touch them.

Nightmare

I was scared to death of what I might find. I formed a U-shape with my thumb and pointing finger and tried to force my eyes open.

They seemed to be glued shut.

"God, what's wrong with my eyes! What did they do to me?"

"Maybe I hit my head on the floor. Maybe the fall and losing consciousness had made me blind temporarily."

I felt a stream of wetness on my cheeks and a salty taste in my mouth. At first I thought it was tears. After a few seconds, I recognized it as the unmistakable taste of my own blood.

I touched my eyelids with my pointing fingers.

I gasped because I realized they were a source of the blood. My heart pounded so hard against my chest that I thought it was going to burst.

I tried to stand up, but I felt so cold and nervous that I could hardly move. I started to shake uncontrollably. The room started spinning as I struggled to breathe.

I rubbed the front of my neck with my right hand, wondering if the attackers had cut my throat because my neck was so sore.

As I did so, my arm rubbed against my bare skin and I realized that I wasn't wearing my dress anymore. I felt my right thigh. I was still wearing a slip but my panties were gone.

"Oh, God, please help me! What is happening to me?"

The thought that Ronnie's friends had raped me and put something in my eyes filled me with terror.

All I could think to do was scream. I screamed as loudly as I could, hoping someone would hear me.

I screamed until my chest hurt and I was short of breath. After resting for a second, I screamed again.

I kept thinking and hoping that if I screamed loud enough that God would make the nightmare end and I would be able to see again.

I tried to feel my way around the room but I kept tripping over things like the coffee table, the crib, and toys.

The room spun faster and faster. It made me so nauseous that I started vomiting.

After screaming for what seemed like an eternity, I heard a noise inside the apartment.

Maybe the strangers were still in the house. Where were the babies? Why were they so quiet?

"Oh, my God! "They probably killed them and left me for dead, too."

I tried to crawl to the telephone table in the living room to call the police. Everything in the room seemed out place, as though someone had ransacked the house. I bumped into the cocktail table that had somehow gotten turned upside down.

As I entered the bedroom on my hands and knees, I hit my face on the bed because someone had knocked the top mattress sideways.

Maybe I imagined the noise. I froze for a moment, listening for signs of life in the apartment. Nothing.

I reached for the telephone but it was gone. Maybe they ripped it out of the wall. I screamed for help again. If I don't get help soon, I thought, I'm going to bleed to death.

"God, what is going on? Why are you doing this to me?"

I tried to find my way to the bathroom, thinking that if I could see myself in the mirror everything would make sense.

"Maybe if I wash my face it would remove the hardened material from my eyes. Maybe the cold water will wake me up and I'll be able to see again and get dressed and check on the babies and . . ."

My thoughts were racing so fast that I thought I was going crazy.

I tried to stop crying, but the harder I tried, the more I cried.

"Why can't anyone hear me?"

I tried to feel my way to the baby's crib again but now I couldn't even remember where the bedroom was. The small apartment felt like a gigantic maze.

Suddenly, I remembered that Devannie was on the sofa with me before I lost consciousness. I tried to make it back to the living room but I tripped over a lamp and stepped in my own vomit.

The swirling room made it difficult for me to find my way back to the living room. When I finally made it, Devannie was gone. They must have taken her.

As I paused for breath, I finally heard something other than the sound of my own terror.

My nine-year-old cousin Herbert was knocking on the door and yelling my name. I had lost track of time and had no idea that it was late enough for school to be out.

I tried to find the door but I couldn't. The room spun faster and faster.

Herbert cried loudly as he begged me to open it.

"I can't find the knob! I can't see anything! Herbert, go get help! Go get Ms. Simmons!"

I heard him screaming her name as he banged on her door. It seemed to go on forever. I knew she was at home because she was taking sick leave today.

"She won't open the door," Herbert cried. "She's gonna call the police."

Why won't she open her door? Can't she hear me screaming?

Since she wouldn't open the door, I wondered if she really planned to call the police. Maybe she knew something about why I couldn't see.

Why won't she help me?

"Herbert, go downstairs and see if you can find somebody to help me! Tell somebody to please call the police!"

I tried finding the babies one minute and finding a place to hide the next. What if my tormentors came back to kill me before help arrived?

As I heard Herbert go down the steps, I thought I might die before he made it back. What if they were still outside and grabbed him?

I crawled to the living room window facing the street. Once I felt the curtain, I stood up and rammed my elbow into the glass, breaking it.

"Somebody, help me, please!"

Moments later, I heard voices and footsteps outside the front door.

"Open the door!" a man shouted. "This is the police."

"I don't know how," I cried. "I can't see!"

Within seconds, they broke through the front door and rushed inside to help me.

"I can't see! I can't see!"

"Je-e-sus Christ!" someone said.

"Go to the car and tell 'em to get an ambulance here quick," he said to someone else in the room. He grabbed my bathrobe and helped me put it on.

When the other man returned, I could hear them asking me questions but I was unable to answer. There seemed to be a barrier between us.

"Lord, have mercy!" Ms. Simmons shrieked and as she began crying. I didn't even hear her come into the apartment.

Her reaction told me that something terrible had happened to me. At that moment, I lost my grip on reality.

My spirit floated above the two police officers. It watched them as they held me by my arms and escorted me downstairs, and it flew over them as they put me inside their police car.

CHAPTER 2

Flashback

"This is Badge 6604 in Car 702," Officer Jerome Dampier said over the crackling radio.

"We have a black female subject, approximately 16 to 19 years old, rescued from Apartment 3-West at 5782 Kingsbury. Victim is bleeding from both eyes and in a semiconscious state."

"Repeat . . . victim is in shock and is unable to respond to questioning."

"Remaining on the scene to search the premises for other possible victims and to interview witnesses. Subject is being transported to City Number Two. Over."

"Roger that," the dispatcher replied.

Dampier rushed back upstairs to examine the apartment.

Jotting down notes as he walked around, his first impression was that the victim had thrown a party where things got out of hand.

He pinched his nostrils periodically and watched his step because vomit was everywhere.

He assumed that she had consumed too much liquor and that a male or males had raped her because the sofa pillows were on the floor and the only thing the girl had on was a slip. He noted several spots of blood on her housecoat, the bedspread and the sheet.

"Victim should be checked for evidence of rape," he wrote on his pad.

As he entered the master bedroom, he noticed that the mattress was halfway off the bed.

To his left was an infant asleep in a crib. Upon entering the second bedroom, he saw another child sleeping.

He opened the bathroom door and looked around. There were nothing unusual, but he saw pieces of a broken glass near the toilet and under the sink.

The sink was clean.

He also saw a broken glass mug in the trash can. It had the familiar "Steak 'n Shake" logo stenciled on it.

Although he didn't move the glass because he wanted crime scene investigators to inspect the place first, he noticed that a large curved shard was missing.

After checking the kitchen and inside the closets, Dampier left and went to Apartment 3-East to interview Ms. Simmons.

Bettye Simmons was the woman who called 911. She was waiting for him on the third floor landing when he and partner Oliver Ising arrived.

"There's some babies still inside the apartment," Dampier said as she stood in her doorway.

"They seem to be okay. In fact, they're still sleeping . . . Would you mind keeping them until we can contact the parents? Otherwise, we have to turn them over to child protection services."

"No, not at all," Ms. Simmons said.

Dampier and Ising returned to the apartment and got the children. Ms. Simmons stood in the doorway, looking inside as they came out of the bedrooms. They followed her back to her apartment.

"What did the girl say happened in there?" Dampier asked as he handed the infant to her.

"She didn't say anything. Her little cousin came over and knocked on my door and told me that Pat was in trouble."

"What's her name?"

"Her name is Wilma Chestnut, but everybody calls her Pat."

7

"Where's the cousin?"

"That's him down there," Simmons said, pointing to nine-year-old Herbert Harry.

"Herbert, come here, baby," she said.

Herbert was standing near the corner of the three-story apartment building, crying. He watched while medics worked on Wilma inside the ambulance. Seeing blood dripping from Wilma's eyes was worse than anything he had ever seen on television.

He trembled as the gigantic-looking officer stared at him. Sensing the boy's fear, Dampier smiled at him while walking down the steps. Upon reaching him, Dampier crouched down to establish eye contact.

"Hello, Herbie. My name is Officer Dampier. I'm trying to find out what happened to Wilma. Can you help me? Do you know how she got hurt?"

"No, Sir," he answered nervously. "I didn't do nothing to her. She was crying when I came home from school, so I told Ms. Simmons to call 911."

Amused that Herbert considered himself a suspect, Dampier flashed a big grin and chuckled.

"Aw, Herbie," he said, "I know you didn't do anything. Did you see anybody leaving the apartment when you came home from school? "

"When I came home for lunch, there were three men in my house talking to her."

"You mean Wilma, right?"

"Yes, sir."

"What were they doing? We're they drinking beer or something?"

"No, Sir," Herbert replied. "Wilma gave one of 'em a glass of water but wasn't nobody drinking beer or nothing."

"She told them that they had to leave because she was tired. So they left, and then Wilma gave me a dime so I could buy some candy from the Candy Lady on my way back to school."

"Do you know the men's names, Herbie?" Dampier asked. "We're they young or old?"

"I think one of the 'em was a teenager and the other ones was grown, but I don't know their names. I never saw them before."

"How many of them was it?"

"Three. It was three of 'em"

"Okay, Herbie," he continued. "That's very helpful. So what happened when you came home from school?"

Herbert said that when he opened the front entrance to the six-unit apartment building, he heard someone screaming.

"I knew it was Wilma," he said, because as he neared the entrance he saw one of the three visitors running toward the rear of the building.

Herbert said he dashed upstairs after waiting for a minute to make sure no one else was coming out of his apartment. He saw a pair of pink panties on the second floor landing.

He assumed that they belonged to Wilma, he said, because she was wearing a pink slip under her bathrobe that morning as she fixed breakfast. After knocking on the door and hearing Wilma scream again, he asked Ms. Simmons to call the police.

"I kept telling Miss Simmons that something was wrong with Pat, but she wouldn't open the door. All she said was that she would call the police. So I started walking downstairs to go find somebody to help her and that's when y'all came."

"Do you think that you could recognize the dudes?" Dampier asked.

"Uh, I think so," he answered.

A troubled look suddenly came over his face as he wondered whether the men might come back and hurt him, too.

"I'm not sure," Herbert added.

"No problem," Dampier said. "Maybe we can talk about it later."

During a search of the apartment, Dampier found a small black purse containing Wilma's identification card from Beaumont High School. The card also listed her home address as 3806 Newstead Avenue.

After Dampier got into the car, Ising turned on the cruiser's emergency lights and siren.

Just as the officers were about to pull off, Lillie Harry and her friend drove up.

"Oh, my God!" What in the world is going on?"

A million bad thoughts ran through her mind as Herbert dashed toward the car.

"Momma," he shouted, "something happened to Pat and they 'bout to take her to the hospital!"

"Where are the babies?" Lillie asked him as she exited the car and headed for the ambulance.

"They're upstairs with Ms. Simmons," Herbert said. "She told the police that she would watch them until y'all came home."

Lillie approached the ambulance. The doors were still open and she could see the medics doing something to Wilma's face and placing a needle in her arm.

"Oh, my God, what's wrong with her?" she asked them.

"Are you the parent?" a medic responded.

"No, I'm her cousin," Lillie said. "She was watching my kids."

"Lillie! Lillie!" Wilma shouted.

"It's okay, baby, I'm here."

"I want to ride with you all to the hospital but I need to check on my babies first," she told the driver.

"We're leaving in a minute, ma'am. Make it fast, real fast" the medic warned.

As Lillie entered the apartment building, Ms. Simmons headed down the steps to let her know that the kids were all right.

"They're still sleeping. Go on to the hospital. The kids are fine."

Lillie exited the building and ran toward the ambulance. A medic quickly closed the doors after Lillie hopped in. He tapped on the panel behind the driver's head as a signal to take off.

By the time the ambulance departed, Dampier and Ising were driving past Holy Rosary School, located a few yards from Wilma's house. They turned off the lights and siren and double-parked the car. The trip from Kingsbury had only taken them about fifteen minutes.

Wilma lived with her mother, her stepsister Ernestine and Linda Prophet, a close family friend.

Colia Chestnut had just arrived home from work when the officers pulled up. It was a quarter after four. She knew only too well that a police officer knocking on your door was never a good sign, no matter where you live or what time of the day it is.

"Yes?"

"Are you Wilma Chestnut's mother?" Dampier asked.

"Yes, I am," she replied. "Is there a problem?"

"Well, ma'am," he said softly and avoiding eye contact, "something's happened to her. She's at Homer G."

"We need to take you to her right away. We're trying to figure out what happened."

Colia felt her stomach do a somersault. If Wilma was unable to tell them what had happened, maybe the officers were trying to tell her gently that Wilma had suffered a catastrophic head injury.

"She couldn't tell you what happened?" Colia asked nervously.

"Uh, no ma'am," Ising replied.

"Oh, my God!" Colia said. "Let me grab my purse and I'll be right out."

After grabbing her purse, she realized that her heartbeat was erratic. She opened the front door, sat at the top of the stairs and tried to catch her breath.

"Look, my heart can't take this kind of strain," she began. "If my baby is dead, I need you to tell me so right now."

"If something terrible has happened to her, I need you to tell me right now. I am not budging from these steps until you tell me what's wrong with my child."

"Is she dead?" she asked.

"No, ma'am, but she's in shock," Dampier said. "Something happened to her eyes and we don't know what because we can't make any sense out of what she's saying."

"In both of 'em?" she asked.

"Uh, yes ma'am," Dampier said as he looked toward the ground. "It looks like whatever happened affected both of her eyes because they're swollen."

He didn't mention that they were bloody because he felt that it would have been too much bad news at once.

"Lord, have mercy!"

Colia stared off into the distance. She pressed the palm of her right hand against her chest.

"We're hoping that maybe hearing your voice will help bring her around," Dampier said.

Colia got up and locked the front door. The officers stood on either side of the stairs in case she fainted. They walked briskly to the police car. She cried softly as the car sped away with the siren blaring and the lights flashing.

When Dampier looked back at her through his rear view mirror and saw her dabbing at her eyes, his own eyes filled with tears. He tried to wipe them away before his partner noticed.

No one said a word during the short ride.

The siren squealed as Ising sped toward Homer G. Phillips Hospital.

As they entered the emergency room section of the all-black hospital on the poor side of town, nurses led them to an examination room where doctors were already treating Wilma.

Colia was surprised to find that Lillie had already made it to the hospital but said nothing because all she could see was her daughter surrounded by emergency room personnel.

She gasped when she moved in closer and got a closer look. Wilma's eyes were so swollen that Colia involuntarily let out a short, loud cry.

The gauze that they were using to clean her eyes was bloody and the medical staff made statements that indicated they had no idea of how she could have sustained the injuries.

"We need an ophthalmologist in here, stat!" a nurse with a foreign accent yelled after forcing open Wilma's eyes.

Colia worked at a hospital. She knew things were not good when she heard the nurse say that.

Lillie walked over to Colia and gave her a hug. They both started crying.

"I've been trying to talk to her but she doesn't even know who I am," Lillie said. "I'm so sorry, Colia."

Colia said nothing; the only thing she could see or hear was Wilma.

"Pat, this is Momma, baby," Colia said as she stood next to the examining table.

"What happened?"

"Ronnie . . . Ronnie came . . . nothing . . ."

"Ronnie did something to you?" "What did he do, Sugar?" Colia asked as her heart pumped faster and throbbed against her chest.

"Nothing . . . Ronnie . . . Ronnie."

Hoping to bring Wilma back to reality, Colia called her by her middle name, something she did only when she was desperate for her attention.

"Who am I, Artimease?" she asked. "What is my name?"

"Ronnie . . . Ronnie . . ."

As Colia's heart sank, she asked Wilma one more question.

"Who are you . . . what is your name, baby?"

"Ronnie . . . Ronnie . . . Ronnie."

Colia nearly passed out. She feared that Wilma had suffered a nervous breakdown.

She sensed that the trauma to her eyes was something from which she might never recover. She came to that conclusion after noticing the baffling and frightened look on the medical staffers' faces.

A young resident asked Colia not to ask Wilma any more questions after he noticed that Wilma's heartbeat was rising fast. He feared that Colia's presence was aggravating Wilma already fragile state of mind.

When the ophthalmologist arrived, he asked Lillie and Colia to step out of the room for a minute.

As they left, Dampier and Ising approached them.

They had been eavesdropping just outside the drawn white curtain, but they were hoping to determine who the person was that she kept referring to as "Ronnie."

"Did she say anything?" Dampier asked.

"No," Colia answered.

She stared straight ahead at nothing in particular because she was in a mild state of shock herself.

"She's in shock," Colia said after about 15 seconds of silence. "She doesn't even know her name." She burst out crying.

Officer Dampier patted her on her shoulder.

"Everything will be all right, ma'am" he said. "Just keep the faith."

"Did she mention any names at all?" Ising asked.

"She kept saying Ronnie's name," Colia said, "so I guess he must have done something to her. I tried to tell her that boy was no good."

"Do you know his last name?"

"No," she said.

"I've heard her talking about this boy named Ronnie who's dating her best friend, so it might be him. She said he's a troublemaker."

"As best I could make out," Lillie added, "A boy named Ronnie stopped by to see her. My son said that three boys were there when he came home for lunch."

While the two officers were at the hospital, the Eighth District police station received an anonymous call from a male disguising his voice.

The caller said he had information about a girl who was raped and blinded at an apartment on Kingsbury. In an attempt to get more information, the receptionist asked him to hold on while she transferred his call to a detective.

The caller hung up.

CHAPTER 3

Investigation

Back at the hospital, the ophthalmologist and a surgeon emerged from the operating room with a grim look on their faces.

"Mrs. Chestnut?"

"Yes, I'm Mrs. Chestnut."

"Hi," the ophthalmologist said. "I'm awfully sorry to have to say this, but Wilma has suffered some sort of laceration to the orbital globe in both eyes. We have to take her into surgery to determine the extent of the damage, but right now it appears to be very severe."

"How soon?"

"In about a minute or so," the surgeon said. "You can go in and see her for a second, then you will have to wait in the waiting room. It could take a few hours."

Lillie and the officers overheard the conversation. Lillie walked toward Colia and they hugged each other.

She opened the curtain and walked over to Wilma. She kissed her on the forehead as Colia placed her arms around Wilma and held her as though for the last time.

After Colia signed the consent forms, Wilma was rushed into surgery. She squeezed Wilma's hand and then went to the waiting room. Several hours later, the surgeon entered the room and gave her the prognosis.

"We put sutures in the lacerations on both the left and right orbital globe, and we repaired the right upper eyelid," he began, "so it will be swollen and painful for a day or so."

"Based on the extensive damage to her orbital globes, the prognosis for a full recovery of vision is not good. It's too early to tell for sure, but the severity of the damage does not lend much room for optimism."

Colia knew what he was saying, but her mind would not accept it without hearing the word that she feared from the surgeon.

"So you're saying that my baby is blind?"

"I can't say for sure until after her wounds have had time to heal," he replied, "but I don't want you to get your hopes up because the lacerations are very deep and the corneas have been compromised."

"For now, I would have to say that your daughter may not regain her full vision. She will be fortunate to regain any vision at all."

The surgeon put his arm around Colia as she started crying.

"Oh, my Lord . . . why, why?"

"I'm very sorry, Ms. Chestnut," he said in halting English. "We did our best and we will continue to do everything we can for her."

"Is she still in recovery?" she asked.

"Yes," he replied. "A nurse will come and get you as soon as they take her to the ward."

A nurse came to the waiting room about an hour later and escorted Colia to Wilma's bed. It was one of a dozen on a dark, open ward.

Wilma was still asleep.

Colia looked at the bandages on her eyes and started crying quietly. She kissed Wilma on the cheek and then sat down in a chair next to the bed.

She tried to remain awake, but the day had taken its toll on her. She had been up since six o'clock that morning and now midnight was three hours away.

She hadn't eaten since lunchtime but her appetite was nonexistent. Before she knew it, she was in a deep sleep.

A scream jolted both Wilma and her mother awake the next morning.

When Colia opened her eyes, she saw Wilma touching the protective pads covering her own. They both realized at that moment that the scream came from Wilma, who was sweating and trying to catch her breath.

"Artimease!" she said, "this is Momma. It's okay."

She gently grabbed Wilma by each wrist and pulled her hands downward. "Try not to touch your eyes. Let me go get a nurse."

As she was about to head for the nurses' station, a dark-skinned foreigner whom she assumed was a physician approached her.

"Mrs. Chestnut?" he asked.

"Yes?"

"Hi, I'm Dr. Amin," he said as he shook her hand. Then he looked at Wilma. "How's my favorite patient this morning?" he said with a smile.

"You tell me," she said. "What's your name again?"

"Navin Amin," he said as he moved toward the head of the bed. "I'm an ophthalmologist, an eye doctor. I need to remove your bandages for a minute."

Dr. Amin gently pulled the tape holding the patch over Wilma's right eye. The eyelid was very swollen, so he warned her that she might feel some discomfort.

"Go ahead," Wilma replied. "It doesn't hurt."

He used a solution containing ether to clean her eyes, so by the time he was done, Wilma was in a deep sleep.

The tests that Dr. Amin performed were mostly a formality, essentially checking for infection. The medical team was mainly giving Wilma and her mother time to adjust to the shock of the attack and possible rape before giving them even more bad news.

When a nurse came in to change the bandages on Wilma's eyes, Colia excused herself to use the telephone at the nurse's station. She called her supervisor at Normandy Osteopathic Hospital to say that she would be out for a few days.

"Dear Lord!" the supervisor said when she heard the reason.

"Take as much time off as you need. Is there anything we can do?"

"Just tell everyone to pray for my child," she said.

After hanging up, Colia called home to see whether Linda was there.

She figured that Linda knew Ronnie's last name or would know how to contact Laura, the girl he was dating.

Linda said that he didn't know his last name, but she gave her Laura's telephone number.

When Laura picked up the phone, Colia got right to the point of her call.

"What is Ronnie's last name?" she asked.

"Clower," Laura replied. "Why, is something wrong?"

"You mean you haven't heard?"

"No," Laura answered. "I've been calling Pat at home and at Ms. Harry's house, but no one is answering the phone."

"I'm at the hospital with her right now," Colia said. "She said that Ronnie or somebody attacked her. They broke a glass and cut . . . they blinded my baby."

"Doctors say that she might be able to see again with an eye . . . an eye transplant —"

"What!" Laura screamed. "Oh, my God, Ms. Chestnut, I can't believe it! She's at Homer G?"

"Yes, but she can't have any visitors right now," Colia said, "except for immediate family. "I would stay away from Ronnie if I were you because he's mixed up in this mess somehow. I have to hang up now and talk to the police."

Laura immediately called Ronnie's number.

"What the hell did you do to Pat?" she demanded.

"What do you mean?" he replied. "I didn't do anything to Pat. She's at home with the kids right now as far as I know."

"I'm not talking about your damn ex!" she said angrily. "You know damn well I'm talking about Pat Chestnut . . . Wilma! What did you do to her?"

"I didn't do nothing, baby, I swear to God. What happened to her?"

"She's blind, that's what! Somebody cut her eyes . . . If I find out that you had anything to do with this, Ronnie, I swear to God, you're a dead man."

She slammed down the phone. Despite Colia's admonishment, Laura changed her clothes and took a bus to the hospital. They would not let her in because Wilma was sedated.

Ronnie was frantic. He hadn't seen any of the three men he took to meet Wilma since Johnnie dropped him off yesterday. What had they done to her?

Ronnie tried calling Johnnie, but no one answered the phone.

He told his mother that he had to rush over to his former wife's house because one of his kids was sick.

Instead, he went to the Eighth District police station on Deer Street and told them that he they were looking for him.

Since no arrest warrant was issued yet, police had no idea of what he was talking about. They advised him that the officers looking for him were likely on patrol. After leaving his name, address, and phone number, Ronnie left.

As he walked home, he wondered whether the knife that he had given to Johnnie was used to hurt Wilma.

After a hospital administrator advised the police department that Wilma was alert enough to give a statement, two detectives arrived to interview her.

Unfortunately, Wilma was incoherent and sleepy by the time they arrived. Colia informed them that she was so far unable to recall what had happened.

"The name of the boy she said did this is Ronnie Clower," she added. "He was dating her best friend, Laura. Laura said that he lives in the 4400 block of Kossuth."

With that, the detectives departed, went back to the car to check with the dispatch operator for addresses on anyone named Clower on Kossuth. Then they drove to 4418 Kossuth to interview Ronnie, but he wasn't there.

They were informed upon returning to the station that Ronnie had been there looking for them. The detectives finally caught up with him the next morning and took his statement.

"A friend of mine named Johnnie Brooks picked me up yesterday morning from my mother's house," Ronnie began.

After they drove around for a few hours in Johnnie's 1962 Cadillac, they parked in front of 3857 Kennerly where Johnnie lived with his mother. Johnnie was about 30 years old, he said.

Brooks told him to knock on the door at 3855 Kennerly and ask for Earl, Ronnie said.

When Earl answered the door, Ronnie asked him whether he wanted to ride around with them. The 15-year-old said yes.

Earl looked up to Johnnie, Ronnie said, and it made him feel like a man to hang out with so many older dudes.

Johnnie also wanted to pick up a neighbor who lived across the street from him at 3856 Kennerly, but he wasn't home.

The woman who answered the door told Earl that they might find him in the 4000 block of Aldine, so that's where Johnnie went.

As they neared their destination, Johnnie honked his horn to get his neighbor's attention. He hopped into the back of the Cadillac on the passenger's side.

He told Ronnie that his name was Earnest.

They headed for Wilma's house but Linda Prophet, a friend who lived with the Chestnuts, told Ronnie that Wilma was babysitting for a cousin who lived on Kingsbury.

"I have a buddy who wants to meet her," Ronnie said.

Linda gave him the address on Kingsbury but said that she was unable to call Wilma because the telephone was malfunctioning at the cousin's apartment.

Wilma just happened to call home about fifteen minutes later to see whether her boyfriend had called or stopped by. Linda said no, but informed her that Ronnie had come by with friends and one of them wanted to meet her.

"But I *told* you not to tell anyone where I was," Wilma protested. "I don't even know him that well."

Ronnie had been dating Wilma's best friend for nearly eight months. Laura and Wilma used to lived in the same apartment complex on Kossuth, which is also where Ronnie lived.

However, she and Ronnie had only spoken a few times, and it was never anything personal.

Ronnie told police that as Johnnie neared the address that Linda had given them, "I saw Wilma standing on the corner of Laurel and Westminster around noon waiting for the kids to get out of school."

"I'd like to meet her," Johnnie said.

Ronnie called her name, so Wilma went over to the car and began talking to him. She said that she had to leave, but said yes when Ronnie asked her if they could stop by in fifteen minutes or so.

Ronnie knocked on her door around half past noon. After she let them enter, Ronnie introduced Johnnie, but the other guys introduced themselves.

Earnest told Wilma that his name was Louis, so Ronnie figured that was his middle name or something.

"We only stayed for about 15 minutes," he said. After that, he had Johnnie return him to 4601 Enright, where his mother lived.

"That was the last time I saw Johnnie, Louis or Earl," he said.

"What about Wilma?" a detective asked. "When was the last time you saw her?"

"When we left at 12:30," he answered.

"So you don't know what happened to her?"

"No," he replied.

Ronnie starting shaking and sweating when they told him. He swore that he knew nothing about it.

"Then show us where the other boys live," they demanded.

Ronnie got into the unmarked police car and took the detectives to 3927 Cottage Avenue, which he identified as the house where Johnnie lived with a girlfriend when he wasn't staying at his mother's home on Kennerly.

Next, he directed the officers to Kennerly. He pointed out Johnnie's mother's home and the house next door where Earl lived.

He had no idea where Louis lived, he said, because they picked him up while he was walking down the street.

Based upon Ronnie's statement, arrest warrants for Johnnie Lee Brooks and Earl Stanley Harper, a 15-year-old, were issued the next day.

Police stopped by the addresses given for Earl and Johnnie, but got no responses.

The crime wave that summer was as normal and predictable as the heat wave, so it wasn't possible for police to drop everything and focus on apprehending them, even though they wanted to because of the nature of the crime. Suspects in non-homicide cases were given low priority.

A hundred rumors swirled about Wilma's neighborhood. No one knew for sure what had happened, but busybodies had called the hospital and gotten information by pretending to be her relatives.

A few neighbors had actually gone to the hospital after Linda refused to tell them anything. They went to the admission's desk and simply asked where they could find Wilma Chestnut.

A few who sneaked into Homer G. and made it to the ward were shocked to see her that way. As they neared the bed, Colia recognized them as kids from her neighborhood and ordered them to leave.

By dawn the next day, word on the grapevine was that police were looking for a white man who had attacked a black girl and cut her eyes out.

The real pressure to find Wilma's attackers came in the middle of the week as the latest editions of black newspapers hit the newsstands.

People were afraid that whoever attacked her might be a lunatic who was collecting the eyes of his victims.

Police made multiple daily visits to the addresses given for Johnnie and Earl.

When police revisited Earl's house on September 29, the teenager answered the door. Police advised him of his rights and told his mother, Carrie Leggett, that her son was under arrest.

They drove them to the Juvenile Detention Center and handed custody of Earl over to them. After reading the Miranda rights to Earl once more, police asked him for his version of what happened to Wilma.

Earl said that he, Ronnie, Johnnie, and Louis went to the apartment where Wilma was babysitting because Ronnie wanted to introduce Johnnie to her.

They all left after fifteen minutes, however, because Ronnie wanted to go by his mother's house in the 4600 block of Enright. After dropping off Ronnie, Earl said that he and Louis rode around with Johnnie for a while looking for something to do.

"Did y'all see that record player?" Johnnie asked. "That thing was damn near new."

"We should go back out there and rob that b---ch and rape her," he said. Earl and Louis agreed, so the three of them headed back to Kingsbury.

When they returned, Wilma allowed them in after they convinced her that Ronnie was downstairs talking to a girl. They said that he wanted them to wait for him in the apartment.

Earl said that Johnnie asked Wilma for a drink of water. Johnnie guzzled the water within seconds and asked for a refill, Earl said, telling Wilma that he was very thirsty.

After finishing the second glass of water, Johnnie asked for a third. A few minutes later, he requested yet another refill, complaining that he had a hotbox.

Upon finishing the fourth glass, Johnnie stood up and started walking toward the front door. Assuming that they were leaving, Earl said, he stood and up and followed Johnnie.

However, Earl said that Johnnie suddenly started choking Wilma. She grabbed Johnnie's wrists. Just as she had nearly broken his grip, Earl intervened.

"I grabbed her by the left arm and placed my right hand over her eyes," he confessed as his mother listened in horror and shame. "She fainted and fell to the floor. She was unconscious."

Johnnie ordered him and Louis to take the record player and the cassette recorder to his car and come back later to pick him up. They followed his instructions.

"Don't worry about her telling what happened," Johnnie said as Louis and Earl stood at the front door.

"I'll fix her when I leave."

Johnnie gave Earl his car keys. After placing the goods in the car, Earl chauffeured Louis around for about half an hour, and then decided to pick up Johnnie.

They saw Johnnie walking down the street as Earl turned the corner in the 5300 block of Delmar.

As soon as Johnnie reached the car, Earl and Louis noticed blood on his hands. They both decided to sit in the back as Johnnie sat in the driver's seat.

They couldn't help but stare at his hands.

"Damn," Louis said nervously, "did you kill her?"

"No," Johnnie replied. "I fixed her so she won't be lookin' at no pictures."

As Earl and Louis gave him a puzzled look, Johnnie continued: "You know that glass that I used to get a drink of water?"

He paused for a moment to give them time to think.

"Well, I broke it and cut her eyes out and then I [raped] her."

CHAPTER 4

Stories

Earl said that Johnnie took him and Louis back to their homes and drove away alone. He promised to give them some money as soon as he sold the stolen goods. He didn't know what became of the goods, Earl said, but he thought that Johnnie sold them to a pawn shop.

They immediately noted that Earl was wearing the same purple pants as described by Wilma five days ago. They knew because the zipper was broken. They gave him another pair of pants and confiscated the ones he had on.

After packaging and marking the pants as evidence, police turned them over to the crime laboratory.

"What's Louis's last name?"

"I don't know," Earl replied.

"His name ain't no damn Louis," Earl's mother interjected as she gave her son the evil eye.

"This man y'all calling Louis is a man from Texas named Earnest Craine. He was staying across the street from me with his sister, but I haven't seen him in the past few days. Johnnie's people live next door to me."

"You better tell these people the truth, boy," she warned. "I'm tired of all this foolishness outta you."

"What kind of glass was Johnnie drinking out of?" a detective asked.

"It was one of those big Steak 'n Shake mugs."

"Was anybody else drinking anything?"

"No, sir."

The detective asked the question because Officer Dampier thought that alcohol might have fueled the attack.

"Johnnie was the only one who asked for a drink," Earl added.

Detectives advised Earl and his mother that he was going to be confined to the juvenile detention center until prosecutors filed charges.

Ms. Leggett hugged her son as she started to weep. She shook her head sideways as they led him out of the room, wondering what fate awaited her wayward child.

It wasn't until Earl mentioned the drinking glass that detectives contacted Lillie to inquire about it.

The officers who rescued Wilma from the apartment had been so preoccupied with her health that they neglected to collect evidence or to call for a forensics team. An officer came by late that evening to take pictures of the apartment.

The evidence crew didn't show up until the afternoon of September 29, six days after the crime. That was six days too late.

Lillie had instinctively cleaned up as soon as she returned from the hospital. In her desperation to remove any reminders of what had happened to Wilma, she cleaned the apartment from front to back.

She lifted the forty-pound television from the floor and placed it back on its stand. She removed the bloody sheet from the sofa, threw it into a laundry basket, and put the cushions back in place. She took a piece of plastic protecting a recently cleaned coat, cut it, and taped it over the broken window.

After tidying up the living room, she started on her bedroom. She put her bed back together and hung the small paintings back on the wall. Then she went to the bathroom. She removed the larger pieces of broken glass from the toilet and threw them into the trash can.

The tiniest fragments were sucked down the drain when she flushed. Then she put the bag of trash into the outside trash container and moved it to the curb for pickup.

Once everything was back in place, she scrubbed everything in sight with Pine-Sol poured into a bucket of water. Droplets of blood were everywhere, especially on the floor by the broken window.

After picking up her children from Bettye's house, she bathed them and put them to bed. Then she took one of her "nerve pills," and fell asleep.

A city trash truck carted away the main pieces of evidence the morning after the attack.

The officer had taken several photos of each room and the broken window, but otherwise left the apartment with nothing. The crime scene could no longer tell the story, and the key witness was blind.

In the meantime, the search for Johnnie and Earnest continued. As it turned out, Johnnie was already in custody on other charges.

Snafus like this happened frequently. Teletypes and the APB (all-points bulletin) were no match for the fast pace of crime and habitual criminals.

In fact, this would be Johnnie's third arrest in three weeks. He was arrested on September 14 for driving while intoxicated (DWI), failure to have a valid state driver's license, and failure to display a valid license plate. He served five days in jail and was released on September 20.

His next encounter with the police was, oddly enough, on September 23 – the day that Wilma was blinded. He tried to drive his old Cadillac to Ronnie Clower's house early that evening but the car broke down. So he went to Sammie's house to request a lift.

When Sammie declined because his gas tank was empty, Johnnie offered him the change in his pocket, which was approximately a dollar and a quarter.

They headed for Ronnie's house as soon as Sammie gassed up. Ronnie's mother recognized Johnnie as the same man who had come by earlier that morning.

"He's not here but I'll tell him you stopped by. What's your name again?"

"Johnnie," he replied. "Do you know where I can find him?"

Even though she had a bad feeling about Johnnie, she told him where he might find her son. By the time Johnnie arrived at the friend's house, however, Ronnie had already left. Frustrated, Johnnie returned home.

He was finally able to get his car started by dusk, so he drove to a colleague's house to pick up a few dollars that the man owed him. As he neared the intersection of Vandeventer and Maffitt, the car in front of him stopped suddenly, forcing Johnnie to jam on his brakes.

Johnnie's car scraped the other car's rear fender. A black police officer was driving by as Johnnie and the other driver discussed the damage. He noticed that Johnnie didn't have proper license plates on the Cadillac.

The officer was about to write a citation when Johnnie said he was a mechanic at a body shop, and that he would fix the man's car free of charge in the morning. The officer agreed not to write him up if Johnnie agreed to take the car home immediately and not drive it again until he secured valid plates.

After parking the car near his mother's house, a friend picked Johnnie up and they drove to the city's South Side. The friend's car wouldn't start when they returned after a short visit. No one would give them a jump start, so they decided to push it while having the man's son steer it. Unfortunately for Johnnie, the boy made a wide right turn and nearly hit a parked police car with an officer inside.

The white officer questioned the boy behind the wheel. He didn't have a driver's license. Johnnie explained that the kid wasn't really driving, but this only aroused the officer's suspicions. He ran a background check after interviewing Johnnie.

The officer informed him that there was a warrant out for his arrest on a robbery charge.

After reading Johnnie his Miranda rights, the officer transported him to the Central District station in downtown St. Louis. Then he called the Eighth District station (located at Deer Street and Easton Avenue) and told them that he was holding a suspect for them.

Johnnie was taken to the Eighth District station several hours later. He insisted that the charge was a mistake and that if the police would contact the alleged victim, he would corroborate this.

Police were skeptical after reviewing Johnnie's rap sheet, which included a number of robbery charges. Since they were unable to contact the man that evening, they held Johnnie overnight.

By the time the complainant arrived at the station the next morning, Johnnie's blood pressure was sky high. Somehow, police were persuaded that it was all a misunderstanding, so the charge was dropped and Johnnie was released.

Two days later, however, the Eighth District had yet another warrant for his arrest on robbery charges.

After searching for four days, detectives investigating the attack on Wilma finally nabbed Johnnie on September 29 at his mother's house around two o'clock that afternoon. They read him his rights, handcuffed him, and took him into custody. He agreed to talk without having an attorney present.

He gave his full name as Johnnie Lee Brooks, and said that he was born on October 3, 1940, meaning that he would be 30 years old in three days. He still lived with his mother at 3857 Kennerly, he said, but spent most of his time at his girlfriend's house on San Francisco Avenue.

When they asked him where he was on the morning of September 23, he replied that he and a friend went job-hunting. He drove to the 4600 block of Enright, where he picked up Ronnie Clower. From there, they went to Kennerly and picked up a kid named Earl Harper.

"What address on Kennerly did you go to?" a detective asked.

"Uh, 3855 Kennerly," he answered.

"So Harper lives next door to your mother, right?"

"Uh, yes sir," Johnnie replied somewhat nervously.

Johnnie said that he then drove to Aldine Avenue to pick up a man known to him only as Louis. Louis, he claimed, was one of Harper's friends.

After they drove around for a while, they decided to go to the 5700 block of Kingsbury to visit a young girl that Ronnie knew. The stayed for about fifteen minutes. The four of them left together, he said, and he drove everyone back to Earl's house and dropped them off, he said.

"I haven't seen any of them since then."

When the detectives continued questioning him about his activities that day and the visit to see Wilma, Johnnie insisted that he had only seen "that girl" during his first and only visit. He was adamant that he had not visited the apartment a second time.

But Johnnie omitted a key detail which cast doubt on his statement: he didn't mention asking for several glasses of water. Sensing that police were honing in on him as a prime suspect, he clammed up.

"That's all I have to say."

Johnnie was finished, but investigators were just getting started. As they led him from the interrogation room, Johnnie assumed that he was being released. Instead, he was shocked to find Ronnie Clower in the hall standing between two detectives.

"Is this the person you were with?" they asked Clower.

"Yes, Sir" Ronnie answered. "That's Johnnie."

Detectives advised Johnnie that he was under arrest for felonious robbery and assault with intent to do great bodily harm.

Ironically, police quickly realized that Johnnie was facing great bodily harm himself. As they led him into the holding area to await transfer to the City Jail, they had to isolate him from arrestees who threatened to kill him.

"You're a dead man," several men shouted as police tried to figure out where to put him. "Bring him in here," others yelled. "We got something just for him."

Johnnie had been in custody over a dozen times but had never experienced anything close to this hostility. The station house was ill-equipped to handle the situation if a riot erupted, so the chief quickly transferred him to the City Jail.

The lust for Johnnie's blood was palpable, and it wasn't just the arrestees who wanted something bad to happen to him. By the time Johnnie arrived, guards and other personnel had already informed the inmate population that he was coming.

Some inmates had readied their shanks and knotted their sheets, hoping he would be their guest. Others warned guards that Johnnie would not be welcomed in their cells, and that anyone who shared a cell with him would be attacked as a traitor.

Each cell contained a bunk bed and there were a dozen cells on each cell block.

The nearest cell to the guard's desk was emptied and Johnnie was tossed inside. A guard stood just outside, making sure that nothing bizarre happened, like a guard "accidentally" unlocking Johnnie's cell and that of another inmate at the same time.

Despite his isolation, Johnnie found no escape from the constant bombardment of cursing and threats directed at him. Shortly after seven o'clock that evening, he complained to jail guards of feeling ill. He told them that he was diabetic and that he would probably die if he didn't get medical attention soon.

The warden notified City Hospital Number One of his condition. Jailers took him to the hospital around nine o'clock, where he was given insulin and observed for several hours.

They returned him to his cell in isolation shortly before daybreak.

To prevent Johnnie from being harmed or killed, guards considered placing him in the women's section of the jail.

While this was against policy, it was the only option other than putting him in isolation. As soon as they brought him there, the women started yelling and screaming and like the men, threatening to kill him.

To avoid a scandal, the warden put Johnnie in an isolation cell on the sixth floor. The cells were once used to house inmates awaiting execution by hanging.

Johnnie remained in isolation until his bond hearing on Friday, October 15. At the hearing, the prosecutor emphasized that Johnnie had a mile-long criminal record and that there was a good chance that he would flee the state. Another suspect had already fled, he noted.

His court-appointed attorney cited a provision in the Missouri constitution which stated that "all persons shall be bailable by sufficient surety except for capital offenses [murder] when proof is evident or presumption great." He insisted that there was no way the judge could legally deny his client bond.

But Judge David Fitzgibbon surprised the lawyer.

"I'm holding [denying] bond," he said when asked whether his decision was constitutional, "because a case like this is worse than murder."

After the hearing, Warden Alphonzo Lark told reporters that he was confining Brooks to his cell until his trial was over, assuming that the grand jury would indict him soon. "If we put him in with the general population," he said, "someone might hurt him."

It was a good thing, too, because Andrew Williams was among the arrestees.

Williams was being held as a suspect in the murder of Gary Foreman, a man found bleeding to death months earlier on a street near Forest Park. Foreman had been shot once and stabbed twice and left for dead. He managed to crawl out of the park and onto a nearby street.

Foreman's luck seemed to improve when two physicians sharing a ride to work saw him and stopped the car. They rushed him to the hospital, but he died.

Before passing, he said gave a description of a man fitting Williams. Foreman lived down the street from Lillie. He said that "Lillie's old man" was the one who shot him.

Williams had been dating Lillie for nearly a year. Devannie was his child. She was born a few months before her father was arrested. When he found at that Johnnie had left his baby alone in the apartment that way and had hurt Wilma as well, he was ready to kill him. Lillie believed him, which made her that much more depressed.

She was crazy about Andrew. She knew that he wasn't joking about killing Johnnie, which only made her wonder if he had really killed Foreman. She prayed that jailers would keep the two apart.

With Johnnie behind bars, detectives focused on apprehending the third and final suspect, the man who introduced himself to Wilma as "Louis."

His sister told police that he had left the state. Since his criminal record showed he lived in Texas, they assumed that he had returned. A warrant was issued for his arrest there, but detectives were not optimistic about finding him.

Wilma gave detectives a statement on September 24. According to the report (the accuracy of which would later raise questions), she said that Ronnie Clower, a young man who was dating her best friend, dropped by with three friends.

The first one, a scrawny teenager whom she guessed to be about her age, identified himself as Earl. The other two men were much older, and she wondered why they were even associating with a kid. The thing that she remembered most about Earl was that he was wearing a purple shirt and matching pants, and that his pants were unzipped because the zipper was broken.

He reminded her of a lot of young men she saw around the neighborhood. They have one expensive ensemble that they wear until it starts falling apart.

The first man appeared to be about 25 years old, she said. He had an unkempt Afro hairdo and long sideburns. He said that his name was Louis.

The other man was the one that left the strongest impression, however, because she assumed that he was probably twice as old as Earl. He also had terrible body odor and the stench of cheap liquor on his breath. Like Louis, his Afro was crying out for a barber's attention.

"My name is Johnnie," he said with a big grin. He kept staring at her, which made her uncomfortable.

She told Ronnie that they could only stay a few minutes as it was time for her to put the babies down for a nap.

"Damn," Johnnie exclaimed as he took a seat at the telephone stool, "I got a hot box. Can I have a glass of water?"

"Sure," Wilma replied smiling," no problem."

She went to the kitchen and got the only drinking glass available, a mug that Ms. Harry brought home from a nearby Steak 'n Shake restaurant. Wilma filled the glass and handed it to Johnnie, who drank it without stopping once.

Lilly didn't want the kids drinking out of glasses because they had broken too many already. She was afraid someone would break a glass and step on an unseen piece. So she didn't keep any.

"Damn, that hit the spot!" Johnnie declared. "Can I get a refill?"

"No problem," she said. "Anybody else want a drink?"

The others said no. Wilma refilled the glass from the kitchen faucet and gave it back to Johnnie.

"Ronnie," she said, "I was cleaning the bathroom when you all arrived and I need to finish, so what's up?"

"Oh, not much," he answered. "Lo asked me to drive out here and tell you that she's been trying to call you but no one is answering the phone."

"Tell her that I'll have to call her tomorrow when I get home," Wilma said as she headed for the bathroom. "I told her the phone is broken." She started scrubbing the bathtub with Ajax while her guests watched television.

"People can call in but I can't call out."

"Okay, I'll tell her," he said. "So, what's been happening?"

"You'll have to stand by the door so I can hear you. I need to finish some housework," she said.

Ronnie stood in the doorway of the bathroom and they discussed his relationship with Laura for a few minutes.

"I don't mean to be rude," she said, "but I was planning on taking a nap with the babies before my soap opera comes on."

"Oh, that's cool, I can dig it," Ronnie replied. "Watching babies takes a lot of energy. I know 'cause I got some of my own. I'll catch you later."

Ronnie walked toward the living room and said, "Let's split."

They left around 12:30, she said.

The only other person who saw them was Herbert, to whom she reluctantly gave a dime because he wanted to buy Banana Splits from the "Candy Lady" across the street.

Herbert would eat candy and consider that his lunch, she said.

CHAPTER 5

Reaction

Wilma said that she had been napping for about an hour when she was awakened by someone knocking. Since she had taken off her dress before lying down, she put her bathrobe on. The door lacked a peephole or a chain lock, so she had to rely on the sound of the voice on the other side.

"Who is it?"

"It's us again," one of them said.

"It's Ronnie and his friends," another one said.

It didn't sound like Ronnie, but she did recognize the voices as the friends who had visited earlier. With the door ajar, she peeped into the hallway to scan their faces.

"Where's Ronnie?" she asked."

"He's downstairs talking to this girl," Johnnie said.

"He wants us to wait up here so we don't cramp his style. He'll be here in a minute."

Wilma was puzzled by Ronnie's behavior.

"Why did he come all the way over here to talk to me about my best friend, and then spend most of his time outside talking to another girl?" she wondered. "Doesn't he know that I'm gonna tell Laura? I should just tell them to leave and to take Ronnie with them."

She said nothing to her unwelcome guests. She knew that guys who think they are playboys often do dumb things like that, so she accepted their story. Ignoring her instincts, Wilma opened the door and let them in.

Wilma had trouble remembering the details of what they talked about, she said, but she knew that they stayed for about fifteen minutes. She had grown nervous about their presence without Ronnie being there.

She told them that they had to leave because her favorite soap opera was coming on shortly.

Wilma sat on the sofa by the front door and placed Devannie next to her to prevent Johnnie from doing so. The way he kept staring at her made her nervous. Nothing worse, she thought, than a broke, ugly, funky man who think he's God's gift to women.

Earnest sat across the room at the telephone desk. Earl, who sat in a large chair next to the sofa, got up and stood by the front door. Then Johnnie got up and approached the front door.

Just as Wilma was about to stand up to close the door behind them, Johnnie stopped in front of her and started choking her, his thumbs pressing hard against her larynx. As she struggled to remove Johnnie's hands, Earl struck her in the face. He placed his hands over her eyes and pulled her backwards. That was all that she remembered.

Since no one knew whether she was sexually assaulted, detectives requested hospital personnel to conduct a smear test for semen. They told Colia that the results would take at least four days.

Four days of not knowing felt like a year. On September 27, the results came back negative.

"Thank God!" Wilma said as the detective gave them the news.

After obtaining Wilma's statement and the smear test results, detectives began preparing their case for prosecutors.

With Earnest on the run and Johnnie exercising his Fifth Amendment right to remain silent, all the police had to reconstruct the crime was Earl's statement and the statement of a victim discovered in a state of shock and coping with the thought of never seeing again.

Not only had police failed to obtain any evidence from the crime scene, but they also forgot to track down the items stolen from the apartment and pawned. When they finally located the "white house" mentioned by Earl, the items had been sold. The owner kept poor records and had no bill of purchase or sale.

Although it was easy for police to get an arrest warrant on the assault charge, the prosecutor rejected their attempt to have Johnnie arrested for theft and violating parole, citing insufficient evidence.

By the first week of October, the Wilma Chestnut story was on the front page of nearly every newspaper in the St. Louis.

Black newspapers such as the *Evening Whirl* and the *St. Louis American* ran banner headlines. Even the leading mainstream newspaper put the story on the front page. "Charged with Blinding Witness," was the headline in the *St. Louis Post-Dispatch*.

By the second week, the story had run in most newspapers in Missouri, in thousands of papers across the nation, and in many foreign countries. The *Jefferson City Post-Tribune*, for example, ran an item on its front page of October 6. (Jefferson City is the state's capital, but also the location of the prison where her assailants would go if convicted.)

European Stars and Stripes ran the story the next day, and the *Baltimore Afro-American* ran the story on its front page on October 16.

Dr. Howard Phillip Venable, the physician in charge of the ophthalmology department, was an old friend of John H. Johnson. Johnson owned of *Ebony* and *JET* magazines, two of the most respect black publications in the nation. *JET* started covering the story early and continued to do so for the next decade.

Most of the stories featured a photograph of Colia with her arm around Wilma, her eyes still bandaged. After the story ran in *Stars and Stripes*, it traveled like an international wildfire.

The stories included five words attributed to Johnnie Lee Brooks that few would ever forget: "I cut her eyes out."

The photo of Colia hugging Wilma typically ran on the same page as Johnnie's mug shot. In the photo, Johnnie looks unshaven, unkempt and unwashed. In short, he looks menacing.

Interviewed for the television news the day after her son's arrest, Johnnie's mother painted a portrait in stark contrast to what the public was learning from the media.

"My son would never have hurt that girl," Mary Childs said. "He has a little sister himself and she's handicapped. She's retarded. He's always reading to her."

As news traveled, friends and strangers alike wanted to visit Wilma. Church organizations wanted to bring her home-cooked meals and pray with her. By the third week, flowers and cards were arriving from around the country.

When Wilma was feeling down one afternoon, Colia sought to cheer her up by bringing her a box of chocolates. Her timing was perfect, as Wilma has just finished eating lunch and was in the mood for a sugary snack. She eagerly removed the top from the chocolates and ate one.

"Oh, these are so good, Momma," she said. "I'm going to save the rest for later."

Before she could put the top back onto the box, Dr. Venable dropped by.

Even though he was not among the doctors who worked on her in the emergency room, he was the one getting all of the attention in the press. Wilma thought that was unfair to the interns who had worked so hard to save her sight.

As Dr. Venable made small talk with Colia and Wilma, he helped himself to one of the chocolates in the box next to Wilma on the bed.

"Ummm," he said, "these are delicious!"

Wilma listened to the paper rattle as the doctor removed another piece of chocolate.

"These are scrumptious," he said as he took yet another.

"Damn," Wilma said to herself, "this dude is some kind of bold. He didn't even ask for the first one and now he's eating them like there's no tomorrow."

Before the doctor could reach for another piece, Wilma announced that she was putting the box away so she wouldn't ruin her appetite for dinner. After getting the box top from Colia, Wilma closed it and asked her mother to stick it in the top drawer of the nightstand.

As Wilma closed the drawer, Dr. Venable suddenly burst out laughing, probably as much out of embarrassment as from realizing that he had consumed more than his fair share.

Wilma thought that she had been diplomatic and suave, but when she heard the doctor laughing, she and Colia started laughing, too.

"I'm sorry," Wilma said, "I didn't mean to be rude."

"Aw, Wilma, don't worry about it," he replied.

"I was the one being inconsiderate by trying to eat all of your candy. I'm the one who's sorry. I've been so busy making rounds today that I haven't had time to eat and I'm famished."

"Oh, Doctor, I'm sorry," Colia said.

She worked with overworked doctors and nurses everyday and knew that many of them sometimes became so busy that they skipped meals. She was about to fetch the box from the drawer when the doctor interrupted her.

"No," he cautioned, "don't do that! Those things are so good that I'll make a pig of myself. I'm headed for the cafeteria anyway."

"Thanks for the candy, Wilma," he said as he left. "I'll have to bring you another box the next time I see you."

It wasn't until Dr. Venable left the room that Colia noticed a little boy in the bed across from Wilma staring at them. His bandaged legs were elevated.

At first Colia thought he was staring at her. Then she thought the boy was staring at Wilma. But when his eyes lit up and he licked his lips as she opened the drawer, she knew what he wanted.

"Poor thing," she whispered to Wilma.

"Who?" Wilma asked.

"The little boy in the bed over there. He doesn't seem to get any visitors. I'm going to give him a piece of candy, okay?"

"Sure, Momma."

Wilma paused. "Give him two. If anybody else wants a piece, just go ahead and give them one. Just make sure I have three or four left for myself."

Like the box of chocolates, all the publicity about the attack came with unanticipated side effects. A black reporter for a local tabloid went to the house one day hoping to get a photograph of Wilma taken before the attack.

Colia answered the door. The reporter claimed to be a police officer. She invited him in and started searching for a suitable recent photo to give to him.

Then it occurred to her that the man was not dressed like a police officer or a detective, so she demanded proof. The man revealed his true occupation and begged for a photo. She told him to leave before she called the real police.

Until that moment, Colia had been wondering why Wilma allowed herself to trust the strangers enough to let them into the apartment. After all, she didn't know whether Ronnie was really with them.

She trembled after the reporter left because she had done the same thing: trusted a complete stranger into her home. She told neighbors that the man could just as easily have been one of the people who harmed her daughter.

"If you had something like this happen once," she said, "you'd understand how easily it could happen again."

Since only two of the three suspects were in custody, the lack of police protection meant that Wilma's life could be in jeopardy.

Her neighbors went to the office of Percy Green, whose civil rights group ACTION was located at 4145 Newstead, less than a city block from Wilma's house at 3806 Newstead.

They were saddened to learn that Green had begun serving a 30-day sentence in the Missouri Workhouse on the same day that Wilma was blinded. He and William Mitchell, one of ACTION's officers, had been convicted two years earlier of disrupting the Veiled Prophet Ball and they had exhausted their appeals.

News about the attack reached Green within days. A member of ACTION purchased a brand new tape cassette player and took it to Green. By the next day, Green had filled both sides of a cassette with well wishes from inmates to Wilma.

Fortunately for Green, who raised more hell than Mother Jones, most of the administrators at the workhouse were black and were also sympathetic to ACTION's program to remove segregation practices in city government. Even the warden was an ally.

Moreover, prominent black and liberal white politicians visited Green on a daily basis. The jailers figured that any man who could unveil the "Veiled Prophet" after nearly a century of secrecy (the group was founded by the Ku Klux Klan) deserved a medal.

Greene was released for "good behavior" on October 14. He paid Wilma a visit at Homer G. Phillips the next morning. He gave her the new tape player with the recording inside and $57 he collected from inmates who wanted to help pay her medical expenses.

He appointed male members of ACTION to stand guard at each entrance and exit from the hospital, and he also placed guards at each end of the open ward on the floor where Wilma was being cared for.

That was only a stop-gap measure.

Green also organized a demonstration at the front entrance to Homer G. Phillips Hospital. When news crews arrived to determine the reason for his latest demonstration, Green gave them an earful.

"If a white girl had been attacked the way Wilma Chestnut was, there is no way that the police department or the city would permit her to be placed on an open hospital ward with no security," he said.

"Some of the people who attacked this child are still on the loose, yet the police have done nothing to guarantee her safety. Since the police can not do their job, we will stay here and do it for them."

"We want this young lady transferred to another hospital where she can have a private room and where someone can stand guard outside of that room. This would never be tolerated in the county. I know it, you know it, and everybody else knows it."

City officials secretly arranged for Wilma to be transferred to Lutheran Hospital in South St. Louis the next day, where she remained for three weeks.

While the local news media was able to find out about the transfer, they complied with a request from the police to not mention the date or place of the transfer. Surprisingly, no one in the media violated the request; Lutheran Hospital was never mentioned by name.

In fact, the media gave the impression that Wilma was still at Homer G. Phillips, while most staffers at Homer G. thought she was transferred to Normandy Osteopathic Hospital, where her mother worked.

Still, the transfer came with unanticipated side effects. Wilma felt close to home at Homer G., and she was.

Originally named Homer G. Phillips for Colored when it opened in 1937, the hospital was located in the famous Ville section of the city.

Its mission was to serve as the main hospital for blacks during segregation, and as a training ground for black physicians, who were barred from working in all-white hospitals. By 1971, the hospital mainly served poor blacks.

It had become so proficient in handling life-saving medical care resulting from street crime that black residents wanted to go there rather than anywhere else if their life was hanging in the balance.

The hospital was named to honor a prominent black attorney and activist who, ironically, was shot to death on his way to his downtown law office in 1931. He was only 50 years old.

The Howard University Law School graduate had spent the last decade of his life fighting to establish a modern hospital for the city's black residents.

An all-white jury acquitted the two white men accused of killing him.

Blacks believed that his murder was politically motivated because the men ran before they even robbed Phillips. His broken-hearted wife died three years later; she was 49.

Lutheran Hospital was on the other side of town – the "white side" of town. Even though she could not see, Wilma sensed the differences.

Things were more business-like between staff members. There were few black staffers and even fewer black patients.

Life on the ward at Homer G. Phillips was always bustling, and it allowed Wilma to partake in the lives of other patients. The private room was great from a security perspective, she thought, but she really missed the communal flow of the ward.

The major difference was that the staff at Lutheran put her on a strict regimen of pills and a restricted diet. Soul food it was not. It was so bland that she could hardly eat it.

"I was receiving five pills a day three times a day," she recalled, "and they tasted terrible. I could not understand why all of a sudden I needed so many pills. After all, I hadn't received any pills at Homer G. Phillips."

When a nurse came to her room one day with the afternoon dose of pills, Wilma put her foot down.

"Why are you all giving me so many pills?" she demanded to know.

The nurse was taken aback.

"You're not eating, dear," she said. "You have to take the pills because you're not eating enough to stay healthy."

"But," Wilma shot back," I'm not eating because you all are giving me so many pills that they're killing my appetite. I can't eat because my stomach's full of pills!"

The nurse laughed so hard that Wilma started laughing, too. She left the room with the cup of pills. A few minutes later, the dietary staff brought Wilma a menu and asked what she wanted.

"I had the best meal since my hospitalization a few minutes later," she said.

When the nurse returned to check on her, she looked at the tray and said, "Well, I'll be darned. You're right, Wilma. There's nothing wrong with *your* appetite."

"They never served me another pill for the rest of my stay."

Reaction

Before his arrest for blinding Wilma, Johnnie's name had hardly ever been in the news because most of his crimes were petty and inconsequential or because the charges were dropped.

There was a two-paragraph story here and there since his life of crime started in the late 1950s, but his lengthy list of crimes were largely off the media's radar.

Not this time.

St. Louisans wanted to know as much as they could find out about him and how he could do something so evil to another person.

But they also wanted Wilma to know that Johnnie did not represent them and that he was an aberration.

Mostly, they wanted her to know that they were there for her.

Johnnie's demonic action evoked an equal good reaction, one that would forever change the life of a girl who felt her faith was for naught.

CHAPTER 6

Come Together

Scouts, school groups, businesses, churches, civic groups , and even prisoners collected donations for Wilma.

Letters arrived from New York to California, many with biblical passages focusing on the triumph of good over evil. Along with letters, people included checks, paper money and even coins.

People of every age, color, and persuasion wrote to her. American soldiers in Vietnam sent letters as long as three pages. Blind and other disabled people sent words of encouragement.

There were so many heart-shaped boxes of chocolates that Wilma gave some to other patients throughout the hospital.

When Colia's supervisor told her colleagues at Normandy what had happened, everyone at the nurse's station was stunned. No one could believe it, and they all seemed to be in a daze.

Augustina Costa, a nurse who had befriended Colia many years earlier, broke the silence.

"We've got to do something about this," she said. "There is no way that Colia can work and take care of her child. There's no way she can afford to pay for her care."

Costa rushed to the cafeteria and came back with a large empty glass jar. She placed it atop the desk at her nurse's station.

Using a black marker, she scribbled "The Wilma Chestnut Fund" on a piece of "nursing notes" paper and taped it to the jar.

By the end of Costa's eight-hour shift, staff and visitors had filled the jar with dollars and coins. She was about to put the jar away when a nurse starting the next shift asked if she could supervise the fund-raising for the next eight hours.

Costa removed the donations, put them in a bag, and placed the bag in her locker. When she returned the next day, she discovered that the nurse had left the jar with yet another nurse at the end of her shift, and that it was nearly full again.

Costa delivered the donations to Dr. Gene Barbour the next morning. Barbour had known Colia for better than a decade. He made no secret that he preferred Colia to look after his postoperative patients because she was not afraid to act as a patient's advocate when necessary.

Barbour was listening to the radio while driving his wife downtown to a medical meeting when he first heard about the attack. As soon as they mentioned the address, he nearly crashed into the car in front of him because he knew immediately that it was Colia's daughter.

"I felt heartsick," he said, "absolutely heartsick."

When he went to work the next day, he saw the jar and put five dollars in it. Costa asked him whether he could keep the contributions locked inside his office because she was afraid to leave the money in her locker for too long.

He kept the money locked in his desk, but it became apparent in a matter of days that a better system was needed.

A number of organizations, among them the Lions Club, the Rotary Club, the Daughters of Isis, and dozens of others were raising funds.

Barbour contacted Dr. Venable and they agreed to create a formal committee of trustees along with a centralized location for donations before things spiraled out of control.

A comment from Colia and something he read in the newspaper changed Barbour's goals for the fund. On the third day of Wilma's hospitalization, someone broke into their home and stole everything that wasn't nailed down. There was immediate speculation that the assailants or someone connected with them might have done it.

When Colia stopped by to pick up her check that Friday, Barbour mentioned that he was worried about Wilma's safety.

"That's not my only concern," Colia said.

"The men who did this don't live too far from us. They can cut through the park and be at my house in twenty minutes. Plus, one of them is still on the run."

"Dear God, Colia," he replied. "We have to get you out of there."

Barbour knew what he wanted to accomplish, but he also knew that it would take a miracle for him to achieve his goal of paying for her care *and* for a safe place to live.

He was not so naïve as to entertain the notion of paying cash for a home, but his pipe dream was to have enough to make a modest down payment.

He was thankful that at least Wilma was able to enroll at the Missouri School for the Blind without having to worry about tuition. The school allowed students the option of deferring tuition payments until they reach adulthood.

As more and more people called inquiring about where to send their donation collections, Barbour and Venable decided to create two collection centers, one in the inner city and one in the suburbs.

Barbour used his office at Normandy Hospital to store the money until it could be counted and deposited, and Venable did the same at Homer G. Phillips.

Warren Bruckner, the comptroller at Normandy, volunteered to administer the fund.

Several large companies wanted to contribute, and some wanted to donate new appliances and furniture. A few, however, wanted to know whether such donations were tax-deductible.

Kent D. Kehr, an international taxes attorney for St. Louis-based Ralston Purina Company, contacted the office of U.S. Senator Stuart Symington Sr. (D-Mo.).

Within days, the Internal Revenue Service recognized the fund as a tax-exempt charitable organization

On October 4, Barbour went to Northland Bank near the hospital to set up an account for "The Wilma Chestnut Fund." Upon hearing Barbour's mission, the president of the bank was so touched that he took a fifty-dollar bill from his wallet and added it to the donations that Barbour brought to the bank in his medical bag.

The initial deposit was nearly $500.

Normandy also opened the "Wilma Chestnut Office" to handle the sky-rocketing number of telephone calls inundating the hospital's switchboard. It hired temporary operators to assist the permanent operators.

Since calls were pouring in from around the nation, the lines dedicated to Wilma were staffed around the clock.

Eight paperboys from an inner city neighborhood donated all of their earnings for a week to the fund. Their $52 total doesn't sound like much, but keep in mind that they were all under the age of 12 and they only earned a nickel from each paper sold.

A sixth-grade class in suburban Richmond Heights collected $500 by going door-to-door in their neighborhood. Wilma's former classmates at Beaumont High School and at Halter High in Wellston raised several hundred dollars.

Employees at the Charles Nagel Post Office branch collected $300 during the first week of October and collected more than $1,000 a week later.

A local savings and loan offered her permanent employment whenever she felt ready to start.

A week after the story broke, Wilma was receiving an average of 40 pieces of mail every day. Colia would deliver only a small portion of it to her, however, to avoid Wilma being overwhelmed by it all.

While Colia and hospital staff members read some of the letters to her, Barbour also recruited student volunteers.

When the minuscule mailroom staff at both Homer G. Phillips and Normandy complained that it was impossible for them to handle the volume of letters and boxes addressed to Wilma, Dr. Barbour opened a post office box in her name and had the postal service redirect all mail addressed to her at the hospitals.

One of the letters that Wilma treasured most was in Braille. Although Wilma was learning the ELAN system (Enlarged Letters And Numbers in raised type), a nurse who understood Braille read the letter to her.

"I am 17 years old like you," he wrote, "and have been blind since I was a baby. I'm sure you will have many memories of the things you have seen."

"There are lots of things we can do, a lot more than people realize . . . So all I can say is 'welcome to my world. It, too, can be beautiful. It's up to you.'"

"That letter gave me so much hope," she said.

A fifth grader wrote an equally touching letter. After expressing how sorry he was for the way she had been hurt, the boy said that he was praying for her. "I wouldn't like to live any place else in the world unless I could come and live with you," he wrote.

In a postscript, he added: "I am a white person. I hope that doesn't matter."

The Missouri School for the Blind mailed several modified board games and playing card games to Wilma, along with dozens of "talking books."

Another heartfelt letter came from a Tennessean who was serving time at the City Workhouse following a theft conviction.

"I have been down here almost two years," he wrote. "I read that Wilma Chestnut had both of her eyes destroyed and I would like to donate one of my eyes to her if possible."

He was the first of many people around the country who were willing to sacrifice an eye in order to help Wilma see again.

While some were prisoners who were perhaps seeking spiritual redemption, offers also came from suburban homemakers who voiced the hope that someone might do the same for their children if need be.

A wealthy widow from Ladue included a check for $500 inside a letter to Wilma. She wrote that she wanted to give Wilma one of her eyes as soon as doctors could perform the operation.

Others wrote that they were doing so because they were having trouble believing that one person could do something so unfathomable to another. Most of them wanted to assure Wilma that God was in her corner and that goodness would triumph over the evil done to her.

Brook Norton, a man serving time in the Florida State Prison at Raiford, wrote an sympathetic letter sent with a few dollars.

"Enclosed please find my small contribution. I only wish that it could be a blank check. However, my only means of acquiring money is by hand-rolling cigarettes and selling them to other inmates."

A group of U.S. Olympic track team hopefuls held a marathon for Wilma. Each runner was required to find a sponsor willing to donate $25 to the Wilma Chestnut Fund. They collected more than $500 in two weeks.

After a newspaper in Frankfurt, Germany ran a story about Wilma in late October, a German radio station called Normandy and asked to speak to Barbour.

As fate would have it, Barbour spoke German fluently. The interview lasted for about 30 minutes.

Two weeks later, Barbour received letters from several schools in Germany. Each letter included a small donation, but it made a big impression on Barbour and everyone else he told about it. Wilma and Colia both cried when he read some of the letters to them.

Many wanted to buy her a new record player or cassette recorder. A couple of people had already done so and mailed them to the hospitals. To stem the tide of gifts, charities asked people to make monetary donations instead.

In his opening statement during a press conference held at the Homer G. on October 6, Dr. Venable answered the question on the public's mind: Was there any chance that Wilma would ever see again?

"Wilma's only hope for sight is a complete orbital transplant," he said. "While such an operation is not possible today, it may be possible within the next five years."

Despite the bleak outlook for now, he added, there was nothing to prevent Wilma from living a fulfilling life. Arrangements were being made for Wilma to attend the Missouri School for the Blind, he noted.

"Wilma is a very strong-willed person. She has the spirit of a fighter and has already made tremendous progress. She's even learned how to use the telephone to call her friends and catch up on the latest gossip."

Many would have fallen into a deep depression under the circumstances, but not Wilma. Venable was not exaggerating about her resilience. When she sensed gloom from visitors, she would do something to lighten the mood.

She would challenge someone to a game of checkers, which she played with specially designed round and square pieces.

She would have visitors laughing hysterically by recounting a practical joke she played on her maternal grandmother. Lova Jefferson had taken a Greyhound bus from Mississippi and had arrived in St. Louis on October 3.

Wilma knew that Grandma Jefferson was worried about her emotional well-being, she told her audience, so she called home "the other night to reassure Grandma" that she was okay. Using a fake accent, Wilma pretended to be a tax collector.

She asked whether the person on the other end was "Miss Lova Jefferson."

When her grandmother said yes, Wilma said that they had been tracking her down "about those back taxes you owe."

Imitating her grandmother, Wilma began stammering and stuttering as she quoted her grandmother's response. When the crowd burst out laughing, Wilma laughed until her sides ached.

She was also enthusiastically participating in physical therapy, and she was adept at finding her way around the ward. Other patients considered her a source of inspiration.

Colia, however, had run herself ragged. She was trying to avoid missing too many days of work since she did not receive paid sick leave, and she tried to stay with Wilma as much as possible.

She would leave work at three o'clock and go straight to the hospital, where she stayed until midnight.

She arrived at work at seven o'clock feeling so tired and depressed that it became difficult for the staff to communicate with her. She seemed to be in a daze most of the time.

Dr. Barbour feared that she would suffer a nervous breakdown soon if the hospital didn't do something to help her.

"It's just too much for one person to handle," he told the hospital's manager during a secret meeting.

"Her behavior has changed. She's not the same cheerful Colia that we've grown to love over the years. She's in shock over her daughter and we're all afraid that she's going to collapse if we don't intervene."

After the meeting, Barbour called Colia and told her that he had good news. She would receive her regular salary but was only required to work two days a week until Wilma was released from the hospital.

The hospital was going to pay her for the other days but was assigning her to a single patient: Wilma.

Grandma Jefferson would stay with Wilma on the two days that Colia worked and she would watch the house the rest of the time.

Even with the lighter load, the staff at Normandy noticed that Colia seemed emotionally detached. She rarely smiled anymore and getting her to talk was difficult.

"The light in her eyes was gone," Barbour said.

Colia's mood, and Wilma's outlook, improved dramatically after a surprise benefactor entered their lives. Barbour was making his rounds at Normandy on October 12 when the switchboard operator paged him and said that he had a very important call. He asked her who it was, since patients were expecting him.

"It's Sinatra – *Frank* Sinatra," she whispered as she covered the mouthpiece of the phone with her hand.

"Yeah, and I'm Dean Martin," he responded with a smirk.

"No, it's *really* him," she insisted. "At least it sounds like him. He's calling from Palm Springs, and that's where Sinatra lives."

Barbour picked up the phone, waiting for the person on the other end to say that he was only playing a joke on him.

"Hello, doctor," the unmistakable voice said. "I'm calling you about the little girl who was blinded. How is she?"

As Barbour searched for a response and tried to regain his composure, one of the nurses said, "Quick! Put him on the speaker phone so we can listen!"

"I heard about Wilma Chestnut and was deeply moved by her situation," Sinatra continued.

"I want you to spare no expense in taking care of her, and send me the bill if you have to. I want to make a donation today. Will $5,000 help?"

"Yes, Sir!" Barbour exclaimed.

"Wilma's family is very poor," he added. "Her mother works here as a nurse's aide and she is unable to afford health insurance, so your donation will go a long way."

"Listen, you have that hospital mail her medical bills to me and I'll take care of them," Sinatra said.

"And I don't want any expense spared if there is any way possible to restore her sight. I mean that. I want you to promise me that she will get the best medical treatment possible and leave no stone unturned."

Sinatra also promised to arrange air transportation for Wilma and her family if she needed medical treatment at another hospital in the United States or anywhere else in the world.

"Is there anything else I can do?" Sinatra asked. "What kind of flowers does she like? Do you think she would like yellow roses?"

"Yes, sir!" he answered again. "I think she would love to get roses from you, sir."

"Good," Sinatra said. "You have my number. Let me know if there is anything else I can do."

At first, Barbour couldn't think of anything. But as they were about the end the call, Barbour remembered the upcoming ball planned as a benefit for Wilma.

"Well, you know," he said slowly, "come to think of it, there is something you can do. We're having a benefit for Wilma next month and it would really be wonderful if you could attend and maybe sing a song or two."

The 54-year-old crooner let out a quick chuckle, probably because it seemed that everyone but Barbour knew that he had made a very public retirement announcement in June.

He had spent the past several months assuring naysayers that would never perform again.

"You know, Doc," he replied, "I really wish I could, but the truth is that I'm not singing anymore. Does she have a dress for the party?"

Barbour said that he didn't think so.

"Consider it done, then," Sinatra said. "Have her mother pick out any dress that Wilma wants from any store and I'll pay for it. Just keep me up to date on her recovery, okay?"

"Sure, Mr. Sinatra. No problem."

"Oh, and by the way, Doc, don't tell anyone about my contribution. I want to remain anonymous. Otherwise, people will think I'm doing it for the wrong reasons."

Wilma received twenty-five long-stemmed yellow roses from Sinatra along with a card that he autographed in orange ink.

"I know that things must seem awfully bad now," he wrote, "but keep the faith and be strong. I believe that everything will eventually be fine."

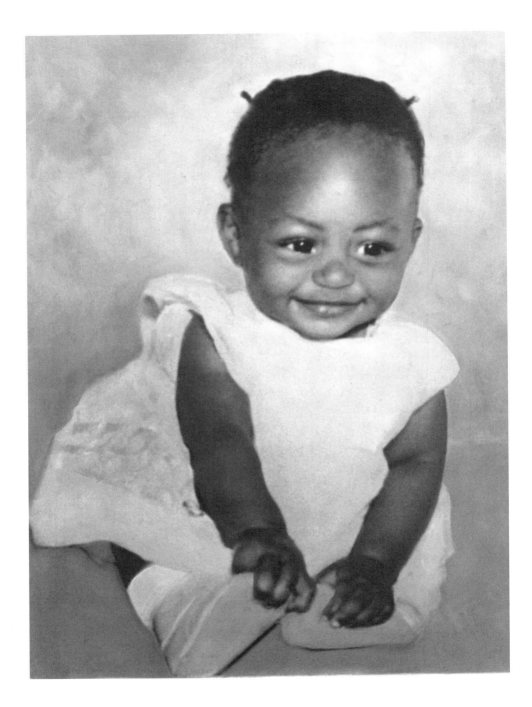

Baby portrait taken in St. Louis, Spring 1954.

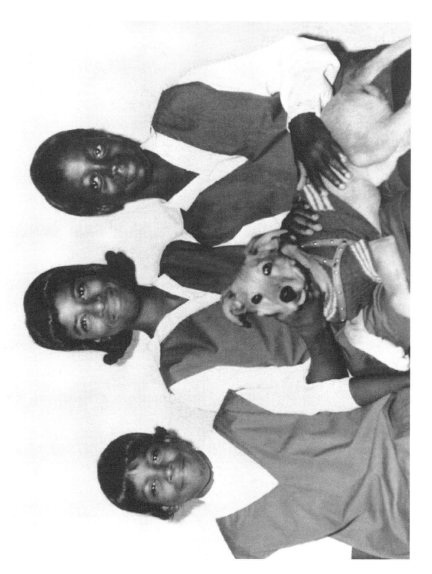

Ernestine, Linda (holding Butch by jowls) and Wilma, 1963.

Eighth grade graduation photo. Wellston Jr. High, 1968.

3. When he rolls in at 3 p.m. in the afternoon full of excitement because he finished all his homework before he left school, or because he has a neat new library mystery to read, or because they saw this terrific film on moon landings at school. I will take time to listen over a glass of milk and a couple of cookies instead of saying "Listen, if you eat all that you won't eat a bite of supper . . . or, tell me later, "Another World" is pretty exciting today and I want to see if Steve and Alice are really getting married . . . or, I can't talk now, I'm on the telephone."

THURSDAY

1:00	Days of Our Lives _ _ _ _ _	5
	Love Is a Many Splendored Thing _ _ _ _ _ _ _ _ _	4
	Newlywed Game _ _ _ _ _ _	2
	Movie: "Mine Own Execution-er," Burgess Meredith, Dulice Gray ● _ _ _ _ _ _ _ _ _	11
	Financial, News _ _ _ _ _	30
1:30	The Doctors _ _ _ _ _ _ _	5
	The Guiding Light _ _ _ _ _	4
	Dating Game _ _ _ _ _ _	2
2:00	Another World _ _ _ _ _	5
	Secret Storm _ _ _ _ _ _	4
	General Hospital _ _ _ _ _	2
	Financial, News _ _ _ _ _	30
2:30	Bright Promise _ _ _ _ _	5
	Edge of Night _ _ _ _ _ _	4
	One Life to Live _ _ _ _ _	2
3:00	Somerset _ _ _ _ _ _ _ _	5
	Gomer Pyle _ _ _ _ _ _ _	4

2:00 PM Central (St. Louis)

ANOTHER WORLD SEPTEMBER 24, 1971

The Marriage of Steve and Alice

Wilma was anxious to get Ronnie's friends to leave because Steve Frame and Alice Matthews were finally getting married on "Another World." After weeks of teasing fans, the show's writers finally let them tie the knot on September 24, 1971.

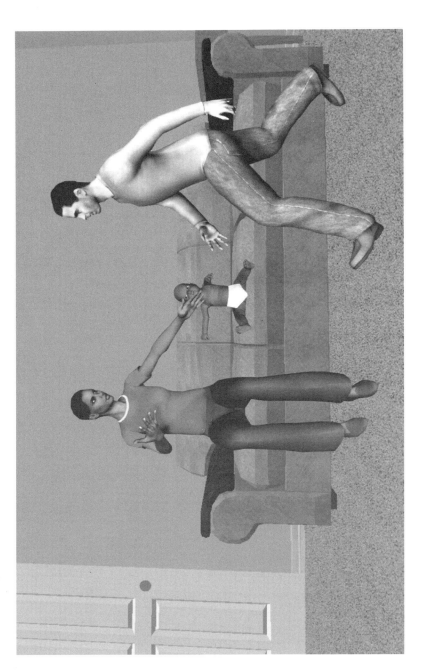

Wilma sat the baby between them to keep Johnnie at a distance. She told them it was time to leave, so Johnnie got up and walked toward the door.

Fair

Jefferson City Post-Tribune

Serving Mid-Missouri for 296 Years

JEFFERSON CITY, MISSOURI, TUESDAY AFTERNOON, OCTOBER 5, 1971

VOL. 106, NO. 31

Election turnout termed 'light'

High height

News in brief

Blinded girl's prognosis poor, hope remains

ST. LOUIS (AP) —

Exchange inmates, POWs

Blinded by ex-convict

Adm. McCain Opposes Any Quick Pullout

Antibusing Amendment Voted Down

House Unit OKs Desegregation Aid

HONOLULU (UPI) — Adm. John S. McCain Jr., commander-in-chief, Pacific, warned Tuesday against any abrupt and unmanaged pullback of U.S. forces in Vietnam.

WASHINGTON (AP) — President Nixon's long-delayed school desegregation aid bill was approved by the House Education and Labor Committee Tuesday but without the ban on busing he proposed.

State Side Lights

● **Plane Had Passenger, No Pilot**

FRANKFORT, Ky. (AP) —

● **Remington Recalls LR26 Razors**

BRIDGEPORT, Conn. (AP) —

● **Cuban Tells of Soviet 'Takeover'**

WASHINGTON (AP) —

BLINDED BY ROBBER — Wilma Chestnut, 17, sits with her mother in a St. Louis hospital where doctors are pondering her chances of seeing again. —Associated Press Photo

Eyes Slashed

Robber Blinds Girl, 17, To Keep Identity Secret

News of the blinding traveled across the state . . .

Suit Against Supremes To Be Heard This Month

BANKERS SCORE NIXON'S POLICIES

The Afro American

UN WARNS SOUTH AFRICA ON RACISM

BALTIMORE, MD., OCTOBER 16, 1971   35 PAGES   15 CENTS

Suspects Blind Girl, 17, In Bid To Escape Crime

6 Catholics turned down in Rome

Mother says money can't undo damage

Pastor chains self to pews in fight against eviction

Wife jumps aside, male

Aid to black

THE LIMA NEWS

Serving Northwest Ohio For Over 85 Years

(88 PAGES TODAY)   THURSDAY, OCTOBER 7, 1971, LIMA, OHIO   VOL. 87, NO. 279   (10 CENTS)

CITY ★ FINAL ★

Nixon To Bare Phase 2 'Teeth'

5% Boost Forecast On Wage

After House Passage

Senate Gets Tax Cuts

New Figures For Income

Tax Breaks For Poverty

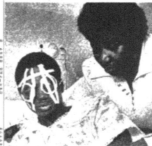

. . . to around the nation and the world.

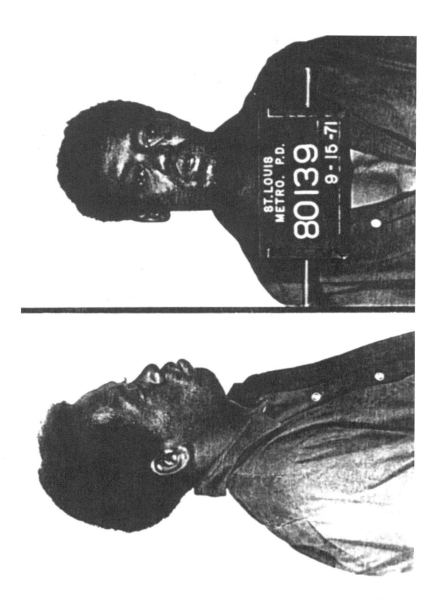

Mug shot of Johnnie Lee Brooks. Note the date (09-15-1971) and his open shirt.

METROPOLITAN POLICE DEPARTMENT—CITY OF ST. LOUIS

CONTINUATION REPORT

FILE NO. - FOR RECORDS SECTION

Two

PAGE NO 8 4 6 1 1

COMPLAINT NO.

Brooks, Johnnie Lee NMS30/DOB10-3-40/Miss./Laborer
A.R.#7-3196   Resides at 3857 Kennerly.

At the time of the arrest, Brooks, was advised of his
Constitutional Rights as they appear on MPD Form #200-19
and he was made aware of the circumstances of the above
matter and he made the following statement:

STATEMENT OF JOHNNIE BROOKS

Brooks stated that he was driving around in his 1962
Cadillac and he picked up a friend, one Ronald Clower,
in the 4600 block of Enright and then went to 3855
Kennerly and picked up a subject known to him as Earl
and then picked up another subject on Aldine known to
him as Louis. Brooks stated that after driving around
for a short period of time he went to the 5700 Block
of Kingsbury and all of the subjects mentioned above
went into an apartment on the third floor and were
talking to a young girl unknown to Brooks but known
to Ronald Clower. Brooks stated that after a short
period of time all of the subjects left and he drove
them back to Kennerly near his home. Brooks stated
that he did not return to the above premises and made
no further statement.

Brooks was then confronted with Ronald Clower who positively
identified him as being the subject who accompanied Clower
and the other two subjects to 5782 Kingsbury Apt. 3W, just
prior to the incident.

Let it be noted that Dets. Kohler and Williams had pre-
viously interviewed the victim, Wilma Chestnut, at City
Hospital #2 on this date and she stated that the three
subjects who were known to her as Louis, Earl and Johnnie
were the subjects who had visited her along with Ronald
Clower and later returned without Clower, however, due
to the fact that she was blinded in the incident, she
could not identify anyone for the offense.

Dr. McKinney of the hospital staff at City Hospital #2
informed Dets. Kohler and Williams that the victims
injuries would probably leave her permanently blind
and due to this fact, Brooks was not confronted with
the victim due to her delicate condition and state of
mind. Let it also be noted that Dr. McKinney informed
the officers that the smear test taken at the time of
Chestnut being admitted to City Hospital #2 to ascertain
if she had been sexually assaulted came back from the
hospital laboratory as "Negative Results".

IF ADDITIONAL SPACE IS NE   USE ANOTHER CONTINUATION REPO

Johnnie denied involvement and refused to talk without a lawyer.

"...They have got Earl down here somewhere. You know I couldn't see hi
if I wanted to. They have me locked up in a place it's no one in there but
me and some old mattress and pillow and other junk and it is really cold
in here. Even if I could see him I would just ask him why is he lying
on me like this. I wouldn't try to hurt him in any way..I don't believe
in doing wrong for wrong so all I can (do) is hope and pray that he will
tell them the truth. The lady that seen them won't come forward and tell
what she seen so what is there for me to do but wait. I don't know anything
Him and God only know the one thing that is the truth. If Tilla had of
told me he had the car maybe I would be home now....See if the major knew
what information the grand jury had to indict me on. The paper said they
indicted me on the girl statement and a police statement. I haven't talk
with no policeman, haven' t anyone talked with me but the priest and parole
officer...." Nov. 9

Listed on back of letter, Nov. 10, names of people JLB saw Sept. 23:
"Sammie Edward and his wife, Tate, Mr. Strain, Tilla, the man I were supose
to buy the ice box from, I talked to him about it, the lady that stays
next door to Cheatham I call m m, the man at the laundry matt, Jerry and
his wife, Garry, Net, Barry, James Walker, Mr. Adams, he were on his way
back to work I guess, he were crossing Vandeventer go up Co tage toward
Prarie, he blew his horn at me, Cheatham, the woman that moved in the
house where the man died at there by Cheatham, they were stand on the front

"...I talked with Earl. I ask him why were he telling these lies on
me and he said he didn't tell them. He said Charles is the one. If that's
so well how did Charles get out there. He didn't go out there when I
taken Ronnie out there so who taken him out there. I didn't. Now were it
in the car when the girl were picked up. I know I wasn't in it. So now
who could it have been. I want you to have Ronnie picked up for the accident there on Vanderventer and Cottage. You know, when he tore up the
man's car on the corner there when he ran into the house and went out the
back, the one you were telling me about. You said car were supose to
have been in an accident out there. Have you heard any more about that.
If you have tell me when you come down here...Earl told me that boy Charles
is in California. Earl had some dope on him he said when they picked him
up. I didn't even know he used dope....I can't take any more of this. It
is to much on me. If I knew some thing about this I would be alright but as
it is I don't know anything about is and I am study trying to figure it out
thats why I wanted you to see the major about get me a lie detector test
before I do some thing to myself. This charge is about to run me crazy.
If I am guilty I will take my punishment. I have all ways in the past so
if I am wrong now I will still suffer for my guilty. That's why I ask you
to get you someone else for if I am guilty I know they are going to kill
me and I don't want any one to have their mind on me....You go to Cheatham,

Johnnie claimed that neighbors could prove he was at home
at the time of the attack. Note that he refers to another
suspect as "Charles." Johnnie claimed Charles was a friend
of his neighbor Earl, who was also involved in the attack on
Wilma.

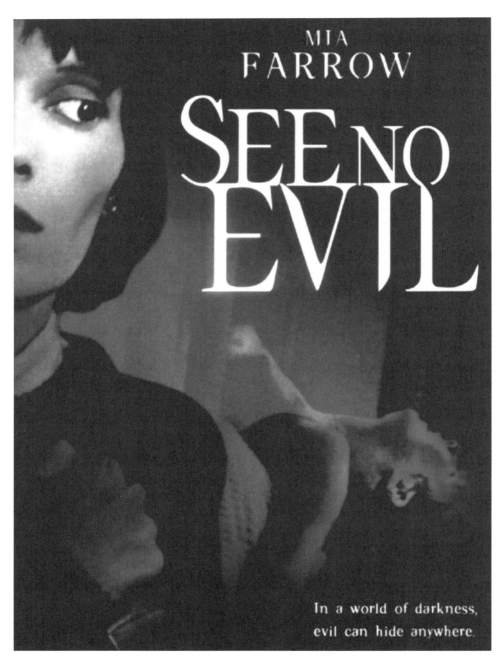

MIA
FARROW

SEE NO
EVIL

In a world of darkness,
evil can hide anywhere.

The blinding of Wilma Chestnut occurred two weeks after the
American debut of "See No Evil," a movie about a blind woman
who is unaware that her family was slain inside their home
while she was at a restaurant having dinner.

The attack on Wilma happened two weeks after the "Longstreet" series began. The show starred a man blinded by criminals who also killed his wife in a bid to escape capture.

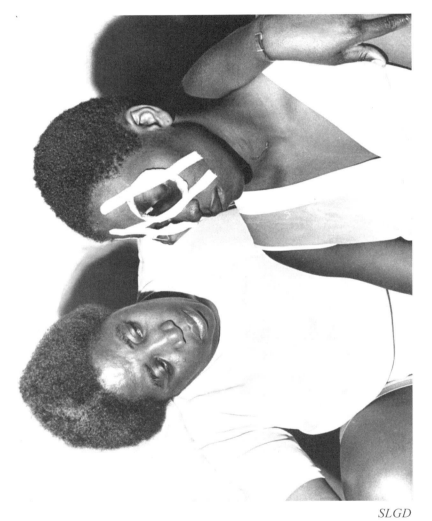

Colia Chestnut hugs her daughter Wilma during a press conference at Homer G. Phillips Hospital.

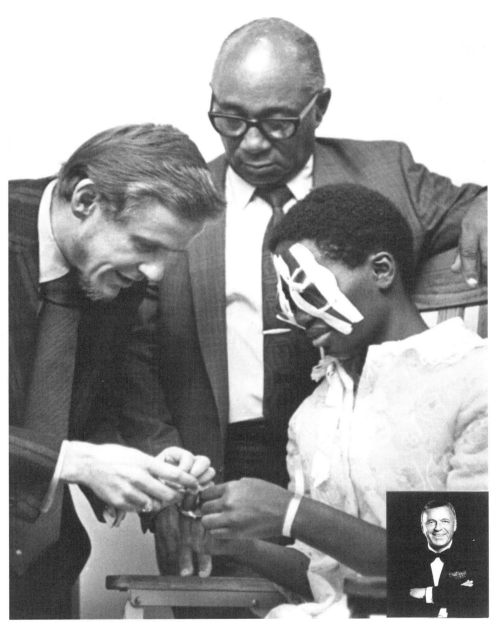

Dr. Gene Barbour fits Wilma with a Braille watch donated by a local bank as ophthalmologist Howard P. Venable looks on. Frank Sinatra (inset) paid her medical bills and was her pen pal for many years.

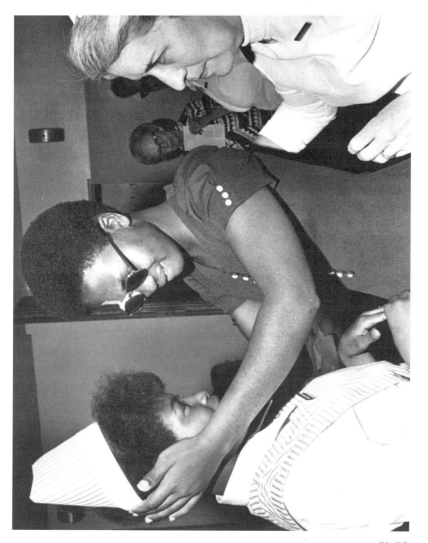

Wilma "caps" her sister Ernestine during a Candy Stripers graduation ceremony three weeks after the attack.

SLGD

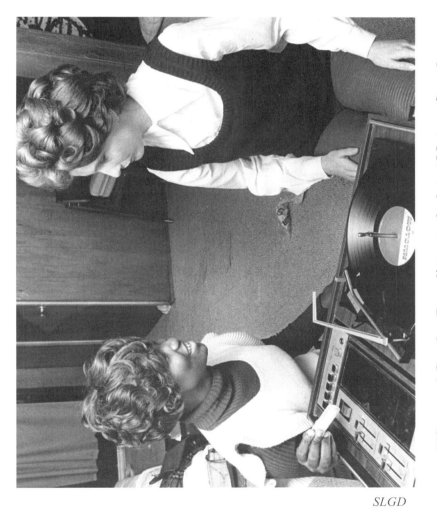

Wilma and Carolyn Renn listen to the latest Motown Sound in their dormitory room at the Missouri School for the Blind.

CHAPTER 7

Cinderella

Wilma got so excited about the call that she couldn't stop talking about it.

"I wish he would have called *me*," she said, only half-joking.

Colia's coworkers planned to throw a surprise party to celebrate Wilma's 18th birthday on October 20, only to find out that it would violate the hospital's security measures.

Undaunted, they did the next best thing. About 30 of them gathered at a nurse's station at Normandy and sang "Happy Birthday" to her over the telephone.

When she received another unexpected call two days later, Wilma thought that it was a favorite uncle delivering belated birthday wishes.

"Hello, Wilma, how are you?"

"Fine," she said. "Who is this?"

"It's Frank."

"Frank who?"

"Frank Sinatra."

"Oh, my God!" she yelled when she heard him chuckle.

"I've been calling your doctor to see how you're doing," he said. "I hope you don't mind."

"No, not at all, Mr. Sinatra," Wilma replied, her voice quivering.

"I hope you liked the flowers and the card that I sent to you."

"Oh, yes sir," she answered. "They were beautiful. I've been meaning to write a thank-you note but I didn't know where to send it."

"Well, I'll tell you what," Sinatra said. "You get better first. There's plenty of time for that. In fact, I would love for you to keep in touch with me so I can keep track of your progress."

"I left my address with your doctor. You write to me whenever you feel like it and as much as you want, and I promise to answer each and every one."

After the call, she started dictating a weekly letter to a nurse who then mailed it to Sinatra.

It is nearly impossible to measure how far Wilma's story traveled, but it didn't take long before even the President noticed. When he read about Wilma and the Richmond Heights class that raised money for her, President Richard M. Nixon personally wrote a letter to them.

"The tragic story of this young girl is a most touching one," his letter began, "and I commend the actions of the boys and girls for the special concern they have demonstrated. Their willingness to help ease the suffering of a fellow human being merits the praise of every American."

Harold Antoine, the social studies teacher who received the letter, visited Wilma and read it to her. During an interview afterwards, he explained why he wanted the children to get involved in raising funds for Wilma.

"Wilma's blinding has really upset the children," he said. "It has made them think about what it would be like to be blind."

It was a question that was on the minds of many because it raised disturbing issues about the role of the media in influencing human behavior.

A study exploring motion picture (television and film) violence and aggressive behavior in children showed that children between the ages of six and nine years old were more prone to hurt other children moments after watching "The Untouchables," a television series which focused on violent confrontations between the FBI and organized crime.

The Surgeon General's Office issued four studies the week of September 15 showing that violence in television programming was precipitating violent behavior among children.

One study showed that children became overly aggressive after watching "Batman" and "Superman" cartoons, but those who watched "Mister Roger's Neighborhood" showed little or no aggressive behavior toward others.

The studies, which revealed that over 70 percent of programs contained at least one act of battery (violence by one person against another), urged television stations to present more educational programs such as "Sesame Street."

The reports were prepared for the Advisory Committee on TV and Social Behavior's official report.

Wilma was blinded two weeks after the premiere of "Longstreet," an ABC-TV television series in which the main character was an insurance investigator blinded during a deliberate explosion that also killed his wife. Like the man who blinded Wilma, the assailant was seeking to avoid prosecution.

In the second episode (featuring martial arts expert Bruce Lee), Longstreet is in the room where a murder is committed, but the case is jeopardized because the blind detective can't identify the suspect except by the sound of his voice.

To prepare for the role of Mike Longstreet, James Franciscus wore a blindfold twenty-four hours a day. He also attended a school for the blind in Los Angeles to get a sense of the challenges facing them. He watched how the students used their canes, and he rehearsed with a white German shepherd named Pax, a trained guide dog.

"It was easy enough to make my way around familiar surroundings, he told reporters. "But once I was outside, I was completely lost."

One of the first shows since "Ironside" to explore the world of the disabled, "Longstreet" quickly became the number one series on television. The idea of a blind "private eye" captured the public's imagination.

Simultaneously, the hottest new movie had a theme foreshadowing what happened to Wilma.

Despite mediocre reviews, "See No Evil" set box office records in America for the week of September 16. Starring Mia Farrow in her first major role since "Rosemary's Baby," the movie's blind protagonist mesmerized audiences as she stumbled through the home of relatives, unaware that all of them had been killed by a psychopath who plans to make her his next victim.

It was little wonder, then, that so many people identified with Wilma. The headlines from both the real and imaginary worlds made it clear that she could have been any one of us.

The Wilma Chestnut Fund was approaching $50,000 by the third week in October. St. Louis mayor Alphonse Cervantes declared October 30 as "Wilma Chestnut Day."

More than 300 volunteers registered. Dressed in blue and yellow and holding canisters featuring those colors, volunteers stood on street corners throughout the city to collect donations from motorists and pass-ers-by.

The canisters showed the same photo of Colia and Wilma that had circulated around the world. Canisters were also placed in banks and business establishments throughout the city.

Local jazz musician Thurman Thomas hosted a benefit concert on October 28, and St. Louis evangelist Barbara Drury sponsored a benefit gospel concert on Halloween. It raised around $500, which several black women delivered to Wilma in a two-pound Old Judge coffee can.

A $1,500 donation from Riverview High School nudged the total toward $60,000 by the end of the month.

A woman chaperoning five fifth-graders representing a group of inner-city schools stopped by Dr. Venable's office at Homer G. Phillips to hand him a check for over $3,000.

On November 14, a group of Illinois and Missouri motorcycle clubs gave Dr. Barbour a check for $918. Two days later, Coronet Dodge gave him a check for $735, most of it from employees and from customers who dropped money into the canisters placed around the dealer's show-room.

By late November, several large donations pushed the fund past the $75,000 mark.

As Wilma eyes healed, thoughts turned to what would happen once she left the hospital. The family was afraid to return to their home. Colia was haunted by the thought of someone close to Johnnie or the fugitive Ernest Craine returning to silence her daughter.

In preparation for Wilma's release from the hospital, Colia searched all over the city for a neighborhood that was safe and within her budget.

Like any mother, she was more apprehensive about the world awaiting her child than Wilma.

"She's not afraid," she told reporters as Wilma left the hospital. "She's not going to give up. She knows that she will not see again until eye transplants become possible. She's planning to go away to a school for the blind just as soon as we get situated."

The "Wilma Chestnut Ball" highlighted the Thanksgiving holidays for St. Louisans. Held at the elegant Stouffers Riverfront Inn on November 28, the event was sponsored by a charitable organization called the Monte Carlos. The ball attracted prominent Missourians and commoners alike.

Life magazine sent a photographer to capture the event for a feature story.

Wilma arrived at the ball in a chauffeured limousine. Her escort, Reginald Smith, was the son of the Monte Carlos's business manager.

As she promised Sinatra, her custom-designed gown was orange. When people commented about the unusual color, she smiled with pride and explained that it was "Sinatra's favorite color."

"He bought it for me."

Over 1,000 people bought tickets, which sold for ten dollars each. The event featured live music by three of the city's most popular musicians: Bob Kuban and the In-Men, the Oliver Sain Soul Revue, and the George Hudson Orchestra.

Kuban scored a Billboard Top 20 hit in 1966 with a song called "The Cheater." Oliver Sain was a highly respected record producer in St. Louis and was credited with launching the careers of Little Milton, Bobby McClure, and Fontella Bass.

John Pankins, president of the Monte Carlos, started picking up Wilma and her younger sister every Friday and taking them to dinner. He would return Saturday morning and take Wilma to his barbershop to shape up her Afro hairdo.

It was a way of putting her in the presence of young men, most of whom Pankins knew would never even consider flirting with a blind girl. Just because she was blind did not mean that she had stopped being a teenage girl who wanted attention from boys her age.

Once Pankins grew comfortable in his role as a father-figure, he started asking Wilma about her relationship with the real McCoy. He was surprised and saddened when she told him that she had never even met her father.

"My parents starting having problems when I was four months old," she said. "My father was in the service at the time."

When their differences became too burdensome, Colia packed her things and took Wilma to St. Louis. They moved in with Colia's best friend for a while. It was two-bedroom apartment in the brand new Cochran Gardens projects.

Praised as a national model for public housing, Cochran was celebrating its first anniversary when Colia moved there in 1953. A decade later, Cochran and its neighboring structure, Pruitt-Igoe, were cesspools of crime.

Colia was determined that Wilma would never return to the apartment on Newstead. Consequently, the two of them had nowhere to go the day before Wilma was released.

The friend who had given Colia and Wilma shelter over 17 years ago invited them to move in once again. The friend's daughter had gotten married recently and now she had an empty bedroom.

She, too, had moved from Cochran more than a decade earlier. The new place was in a respectable black middle class neighborhood. After some hesitation, Colia accepted. She promised the friend that they would not impose upon her for more than a month or so.

By December 1, when Wilma began classes at the Missouri School for the Blind, the trust fund had reached $84,000. The phenomenal success of the fundraising had surpassed Barbour's wildest expectations.

With Sinatra covering Wilma's medical bills, he convinced the trustees to use part of the money to purchase a new home for the Chestnuts.

In the meantime, the combined stresses of Wilma's care, the upcoming trial, the lack of a place to live, and holding on to her job took a heavy toll on Colia.

"The attack changed her forever," according to Barbour.

"Don't get me wrong. She was one of the most positive persons I ever met, and I credited her attitude with helping many of my patients recover. No matter how dim a situation looked, Colia could always find something positive in it."

Barbour and others noticed that Colia was sleepwalking through work, and it showed. No matter what the topic, she would bring Wilma's name into the conversation. This often resulted in her losing her composure.

"It hurt me deeply to see such a good person suffer so," Barbour said.

Cinderella

Unlike many staffers at Normandy, Barbour knew that Wilma was Colia's only biological child. The other two daughters whose photos she proudly carried inside her wallet were stepdaughters.

Colia married Earnest Chestnut when Wilma was nine years old. Initially, he relinquished custody of his two daughters to their mother, but she died in November 1963, less than three months after he married Colia.

He formally adopted Wilma and she assumed his last name. Colia also formally adopted his daughters.

Barbour paved the way for Colia to be hospitalized at Normandy the week after Wilma started school. She was suffering from emotional exhaustion. Even though she stayed for ten days, she was able to hide it from Wilma.

She would stay at the hospital from Sunday night through Friday morning, but would pick up Wilma from school on Friday afternoon and spend the weekend with her at her friend's apartment.

She returned to the friend's apartment on Christmas Eve after picking up Wilma for the holidays. The hospital gave Wilma a German shepherd puppy for Christmas, which they planned to have trained as a guide dog. Wilma named him "Spirit."

While Wilma lived Cinderella's fantasy, it was already past midnight for the men accused of blinding her.

The *St. Louis Globe-Democrat* published an editorial on October 6 that spelled out what many were thinking: the penal system had become too lenient with recidivists, and innocent people were paying a heavy price.

It labeled Brooks a "sadistic, sub-human assailant" and argued that no "man who would commit a savage crime like this can be rehabilitated." The editorial noted that Brooks had a long history of violent felony arrests and despite repeated incarcerations, there had been no correction of his behavior.

Although blacks regarded the newspaper's editorial bent as racially prejudiced, few quibbled about its assessment of Johnnie Brooks.

"We have seen far too many criminals commit a serious crime and then come out of prison in a year or two to commit a still worse crime."

Johnnie's timing could not have been worse. Six women had been raped in a wealthy suburb in the past six weeks and the assailant was still on the loose.

The blinding of Wilma Chestnut highlighted just how far some criminals might go to avoid apprehension.

"Until intelligent actions are taken to protect ourselves from these crime repeaters, there is always the chance that another one will slash out the eyes of an innocent girl or attack some woman on a parking lot."

The *Evening Whirl*, a ghetto chronicle of black-on-black crime, ran a front-page banner headline about the attack on Wilma. The story portrayed Johnnie as a sex-crazed drug addict with a criminal record longer than the Mississippi.

Johnnie had been in the adult criminal system of St. Louis almost from the moment he turned 18. On April 7, 1959, he robbed at man at gunpoint. When the man resisted, Johnnie pistol-whipped him and threatened to kill him. He got a quarter from the man – that's right, twenty-five cents.

When the man summoned police, a detective named Robert Richters gave chase. Johnnie fired at the detective from 20 feet away and missed. He got away but was arrested the next day.

He was convicted a month later of first degree robbery with a deadly and dangerous weapon, for which the judge sentenced him on June 12 to eight years in the Missouri State Penitentiary.

He was also convicted of assault with intent to kill with malice and received another eight years. However, in view of Johnnie's age, the judge ordered him the serve the time concurrently.

Since Johnnie had obeyed the rules of incarceration and didn't commit any major infractions, he was released in January 1965 after serving five and a half-years.

Less than six months later, Johnnie was arrested for raping and sodomizing a young woman. He escaped prosecution, however, for lack of evidence. The woman was afraid to go forward with nothing more than her word against his.

In August 1966, 25-year-old Johnnie and 21-year-old Aaron Clark talked a 15-year-old into helping them strip a brand new Pontiac they spotted inside a garage in the 4000 block of North Market Street. Thieves who were stripping cars had plagued the neighborhood recently.

The old beat-up 1956 Ford and its three occupants looked out of place, so someone called the police. It was also clear from the time of day – six o'clock in the morning – that they were not too bright.

When police arrived, they saw Johnnie get out of the Ford and run to the garage. They immediately placed him under arrest and put him in the back of their squad car.

Knowing that there were accomplices, an officer headed for the garage's front entrance. As he did so, Clark and the teenager ran and tried to escape on foot. They didn't get far.

Police saw several parts from the Pontiac on the back seat of the Ford. Advised that they were under arrest, Johnnie refused to say anything. Clark, however, denied stealing the car but admitted that he owned the Ford and that he had helped Johnnie strip the Pontiac.

Brooks beat the charges on several technicalities. After *Miranda v. Arizona*, handed down by the United States Supreme Court in June 1966, police were required to advise suspects of a number of rights available to them.

When the prosecutor was informed that Clark had not been advised that his statements could be used against him in court and that he was entitled to a lawyer before making a statement, he had no choice but to drop the charges.

Another law held that police must know a crime is in progress before they can legally make an arrest. The prosecutor found that the police failed to prove that someone tipped them off about a crime being in process.

The most bizarre aspect of the case, however, was the prosecutor's determination that police failed to prove Johnnie knew that Clark and the juvenile were stripping the car. This, despite the fact that Johnnie got out of the car and tried to run into a stranger's garage to warn them when he saw police.

On September 25, 1967, Johnnie was drinking at a tavern located near the intersection of Delmar and Whittier.

He struck up a conversation with James T. Bullock, a man who lived in the 4400 block of Delmar, which was about three blocks from the watering hole.

When the man left the bar, Johnnie followed him. As the man neared his home, Johnnie removed a lug nut wrench from his pants and threatened to kill Bullock if he didn't hand over his money.

Bullock gave him all the money in his wallet and pockets – a total of three dollars.

Again, Johnnie had not thought ahead. Bullock remembered Johnnie's name, and he and other patrons had no problem identifying Johnnie from mug shots.

Johnnie pleaded guilty before Circuit Court Judge P. F. Palumbo on November 30. Palumbo immediately handed down a sentence of six years for first-degree robbery with a deadly and dangerous weapon.

Despite Johnnie's long history of violent offenses, he was freed after serving two years. The problem was that the Missouri penitentiary was facing overcrowding from a new type of inmate – political activists.

Black militants were being thrown into prison left and right, and most had not committed a single violent crime.

Percy Green of ACTION and Rev. Charles Koen of the Black Liberators were locked up for civil disobedience frequently as part of a deliberate effort to stymie racial progress in St. Louis.

As a tradeoff, repeat offenders were unleashed after serving less than a fourth of their sentences, and as pointed out by the *Globe-Democrat*, innocent people were paying the price.

CHAPTER 8

Devil's Advocate

During the same week in mid-October that Wilma was transferred to Lutheran Hospital, a grand jury began deliberating charges against Johnnie Lee Brooks. In addition to Wilma, it heard testimony from Lillie Harry, Ronald Clower, Jerome Dampier, and Dr. Reginald McKinney.

Dampier testified that he saw blood on the sofa, on the window that Wilma had broken with her elbow, and on the curtains covering the window.

Despite this, no photographs were taken at the time of her rescue.

Detectives also failed to retrieve the stolen tape recorder and record player from the house where it was pawned.

Moreover, prosecutors failed to contact the pawnshop's owner as a possible witness. The entire case rested upon circumstantial evidence.

On November 3, Judge Theodore McMillan certified Earl Stanley Harper as an adult.

The next day, the grand jury indicted Johnnie and Earl on charges of assault with intent to maim with malice and first-degree robbery.

Many people know that it's not difficult for a prosecutor to get an indictment. However, in cases where evidence is slim to none, the prosecutor has to drum up public support long before trial or risk losing the case.

In this instance, the prosecutor (city's attorney in local parlance) made sure that reporters got access to Johnnie's lengthy criminal record.

Not only did his rap sheet include charges for which he was convicted, but it also included a slew of arrests for which he escaped prosecution.

The reasons had nothing to do with his innocence or guilt, but rather with the lack of corroboration or because the victim was afraid of what would happen to her in court.

Among them were several arrests for rape and sodomy.

While the evidence that the state would be able to introduce in court was minuscule, any potential juror would be inclined to convict him based upon what they had read in the newspaper or saw on the televised evening news.

The combination of pretrial publicity, the barbarity of the attack on Wilma, and Johnnie's troubled past all but guaranteed a successful prosecution.

The media portrayed Johnnie as such a vile, incorrigible predator that it was difficult to imagine anyone coming to his defense. Surely to Johnnie's surprise, someone did.

Alarmed by the tone of the editorial in the *St. Louis Globe-Democrat*, a young Benedictine monk, unfamiliar with the level of violence in the inner city, thought that the media was demonizing Johnnie.

"They were basically saying that Johnnie should be executed," Father Ralph Wright said. "I figured that anyone that bad could use a friend."

He decided to contact Johnnie.

Wright, who received his bachelor's degree from Oxford, was ordained at England's Ampleforth Abbey in July 1970. A month later he arrived in America to join the St Louis Priory, the abbey's anchor school in the United States.

Born David Grant Melville Wright in October 1938, the priest was a country boy at heart. His family lived on the edge of Sherwood Forest (aye, of Robin Hood fame).

His father, Monty Wright, was a fifth generation miner who rose through the ranks to become chief executive officer in charge of the mines owned by the Butterly Company.

The executive and his homemaker wife had four boys, three of whom became monks.

After a brief stint in the army that ended in 1959, Wright joined the Benedictine community at Ampleforth Abbey in Yorkshire. Shortly after joining, he assumed the name Ralph in homage to Ralph Sherwin, a martyr.

Little wonder, then, that Father Wright became a maverick.

His first stop in America, for example, was Chicago. No American in their right mind would have dared to walk alone from Chicago to St. Louis, as the trek would have given criminals and drunk drivers too many opportunities to victimize them.

Wright hiked 300 miles without getting a scratch. A state trooper who stopped him for questioning – anyone would be suspect if you saw them walking down the road at night wearing a dark-colored monk's habit – was flabbergasted when Wright told him the nature of his mission.

Wright's first year of teaching was brutal. The boys had difficulty understanding his accent, and they were puzzled further by how the young priest pronounced his first name.

Although it's spelled the same way Americans spell the name, he pro-nounced it to rhyme with the word "safe." When asked his name, it sounded like he was saying "Rafe Right."

To make matters worse, he was a reluctant disciplinarian at a time when most teenagers were engulfed in the rebellious mood over the Vietnam War era and the counterculture revolution.

The second school year had just begun when the Wilma Chestnut story broke. On October 23, Wright went downtown to Central Lockup and visited Johnnie.

"I'm telling you, Father," Johnnie insisted, "I'm innocent."

When the priest asked Johnnie for proof, Johnnie told him to contact his common law wife, Daisy Joiner, and ask her to show him the clothing that he was wearing on September 23.

"They say that I cut her eyes out," he said, "but you won't find any blood on my clothes."

Sure enough, there were no bloodstains on the clothing shown to Father Wright.

Wright soon became convinced that Johnnie was innocent and that he was bearing witness to a miscarriage of justice.

Even though he knew little or nothing about the details of Johnnie's prior arrests, Wright was won over by Johnnie's impassioned pleas.

After several meetings, the man who had assumed the name of one martyr began to worry that Johnnie was becoming another one.

He told Johnnie to write a letter explaining everything that happened between September 23 and September 29, the day he was arrested.

He also instructed Johnnie to begin keeping a diary of everything that happened to him in custody, including who visited, information implicating others in the attack, and anything else which might help to prove his innocence.

It was ironic that Johnnie, a hoodlum being compared to the devil incarnate, had found an advocate in a priest. It was also odd that the first letter that Wright received from Johnnie was not a thank-you note, but rather a letter of complaint.

Dated October 28, Johnnie expressed anger over being incarcerated. But his primary complaint was that Wright had not received the first installment of his jailhouse diary.

The replacement missive was a 3,000-word account of his activities from daybreak on September 22 through midnight of September 24.

(Since Johnnie asserted his Fifth Amendment right to remain silent when he was arrested, his letters to Wright are the most detailed accounts of his alleged activities. Words in italics become critical to understanding the truth, the whole truth, and nothing but the truth.)

———————

September 22:

He spent the morning of working on his ailing Cadillac, he wrote, and spent the afternoon at an auto graveyard searching for replacements for a bad headlight, a damaged front fender and a bald tire.

He and a friend named Brown spent the evening cavorting at a tavern. The car's battery died while they were inside. After *hours of drinking,*

Johnnie and Brown went to the latter's girlfriend's apartment once they revived the battery.

Brown spent the night with her while *Johnnie slept in the car*. When Brown emerged from the girlfriend's apartment the next morning, Johnnie took him home. Brown's wife opened the door and let him inside.

September 23:

An hour or so later, Brown came outside and asked Johnnie whether he could still give him a ride to the Chrysler auto assembly plant in Fenton where he worked. Since Johnnie didn't know how to get there, Brown drove.

Several miles into the drive, it occurred to Johnnie that he would not know how to get back. They turned back because Johnnie decided to go the home of a friend named Ronald Clower to ask Ronnie to accompany them.

Ronnie was still asleep when Johnnie arrived the apartment. When *Ronnie's mother answered the door,* Johnnie asked her to awaken him because *they had plans to apply for work* at the Chrysler plant that morning. Johnnie was in the house waiting for Ronnie so long that "*the boy blew my horn.*"

[The diary makes no previous mention of a boy being in the car.]

They stopped at a Clark Service station for gas. Johnnie was broke, so Brown paid for two dollars worth of gas.

When Johnnie asked Brown to pay for a quart of oil, however, Brown balked. He told Johnnie that he would loan him the money but that *Johnnie would have to repay him by the next evening*.

By the time he finished pumping gas, the car needed another jumpstart. "I had around 60 or 65 cents in my pocket as I got behind the wheel and we left.

They *headed for Ronnie's house* after dropping of Mr. Brown and filling out employment applications.

9:00 – 9:30: He arrived back at Ronnie's house. Johnnie thought that they were going to Ronnie's girlfriend's house but *Ronnie told him to head for Kingsbury* instead. Since Johnnie didn't know the way, Ronnie provided directions.

Before going there, however, Johnnie decided to go home first. He bumped into *Earl Harper*, who had just left school. Earl asked whether he could ride along with them to Kingsbury.

They went to an apartment there where Ronnie introduced them to a girl named Wilma.

"I asked for a drink of water. I drank that and another one." Ronnie asked Johnnie whether he had a *"hotbox from [drinking] whiskey [the night before], and I said yes."*

Johnnie closed his eyes and rested as Ronnie and Wilma talked. The girl went out the door or someone came in while he was resting. After about 15 minutes, *all three* of them left.

As he drove Ronnie home, *he picked up Earl's friend*. He was going to his sister's house. When they arrived at Ronnie's house, Earl's friend "asked me if I had a knife." Johnnie said no, so the stranger asked Ronnie for one.

Ronnie went into the house, got a knife, and gave it to the stranger. After taking Ronnie home, Johnnie drove home and parked the car because he was out of gas. The boy they call "Scar" [Earl's friend] *went through the alley to his sister's house.* I don't know where Earl went."

After parking the car, Johnnie visited a few people he knew in the neighborhood to *see if he could borrow money for gas.*

He identified a Mr. Tate and a Mr. Strain as two of the people with whom he conversed. Later, a *friend named Sammie* came by to have Johnnie fix his car. They went to Stan's house to borrow a tool but Stan wasn't home. Sammie drove him to another location where they found Stan.

Johnnie also ran into his stepson. He told the boy to tell Daisy that he would be home soon.

He encountered a friend named Melvin and they talked for a while. Melvin was on his way to buy cookies, so Johnnie went with him. Then Johnnie returned to his mother's house and got some lemon drops while Melvin waited outside.

They left and went to another friend's house, Cheatham. Johnnie asked Cheatham for a ride to see Mr. Faris, who *owed him money*. Cheatham turned him down, however, because he was babysitting.

Upon leaving, Johnnie bumped into Mrs. Howard's daughter who was going to Mrs. People's house. Johnnie walked with her until he saw Jerry, another friend. He stopped and talked with Jerry and his wife.

After Johnnie returned to Tate's house, Sammie stopped by. He didn't have enough gas to *take Johnnie to Ronnie's house*, so Johnnie *borrowed a dollar* from Tate.

He bought a pack of cigarettes with the dollar and offered Sammie the change for gas. [what happened to the 60 cents from earlier? A pack was of cigarettes was only 35 cents].

After getting gas, Sammie drove him to Ronnie's house, but *Ronnie's mother said that he wasn't there*.

From there, *Johnnie went to the house on Kossuth where Ronnie spent time*. Ronnie wasn't there, either. Johnnie *bought a quart of beer* with the 60 cents that he had from earlier that morning.

Later that evening, Johnnie tried to find Mr. Faris. However, he was *involved in a car accident* and ended up receiving a ticket for not having proper license plates. Since Johnnie had already gotten a ticket for the same offense earlier that day, the cop gave him a break.

Johnnie got involved in yet *another car accident the same night*. A friend's son was helping him push his car out of traffic when the boy made too wide a turn.

When the police ran a background check, they discovered that there was a *warrant out for his arrest for robbery*. The cop took him to Central lockup and held him for the Deer Street police. Before they put him in the police car on the warrant, Johnnie *"gave the boy a dollar for gas."*

September 24.

The man who had accused Johnnie of robbing him came to Deer Street and straightened out the matter, so Johnnie was freed. However, they told him that he would have to return to Central lockup before all charges could be dropped.

Johnnie took ill while at Central lockup and had to go to the hospital. Since no one was available to take him, police released him from custody and *told him to take himself to the hospital*. They warned him to come back after getting medical attention so they could finish closing out the paperwork.

Johnnie went home first and drank a glass of water with a couple of teaspoons of sugar in it.

Then he *took a bath, his first in three days.* As his mother and Daisy were taking him to the hospital, he bumped into Earl. *Earl asked him why he had been arrested.*

After Johnnie explained, he *asked Earl why he was being sought by police,* too. Earl replied: "nothing."

At the hospital, Johnnie was treated for *bronchitis. He went outside to smoke* after he received treatment [he was treated for diabetes]. When he felt better, the hospital released him. He returned to Central lockup around 9:30 that morning and was quickly cleared.

He returned to his mother's home and stayed there until Saturday morning.

––––––––––––––––

What is extraordinary about Johnnie's letter is the amount of minutiae that he could remember from an ordinary day. Nothing special happened early on September 23, yet Johnnie had amazing recall. How could he be so sure, for example, that he got lemon drops from his mother's house on September 23 instead of the day before or the day after?

Johnnie rarely had more than a quarter-tank of gas on any given day and his car was always breaking down. How did he know how much gas he put in the car on one day and not the next?

The monk asked Johnnie for a detailed account of the days surrounding the blinding of the person Johnnie referred to as "that girl." Johnnie's reply covered three routine days.

His diary for the day before the crime consists of less than 400 words.

His diary for the day after the crime comprises about 400 words, even though he required hospitalization.

On the day of the crime, in which nothing notable happened until late in the evening, Johnnie's recollection added up to over 2,000 words.

Johnnie had such a convincing alibi that his lawyers should have had no problem clearing his name. Since he visited so many friends and neighbors on the day of the crime, finding witnesses should have been easy.

Alas, that was not the case.

According to his attorneys, negative publicity surrounding his arrest made witnesses reluctant to come forth on Johnnie's behalf.

When Johnnie wrote to Father Wright before the indictment, he referred to Craine as "Earl's friend," and "that boy" suggesting that he did not know him.

In letters he wrote a week *after* the indictment, he repeatedly refers to the scar-faced stranger as "Charles."

"Earl's friend's full name was Earnest Charles Craine. People vaguely familiar with him called him Earnest, as one would expect.

Good friends, he would say later, called him "Charles" or "Scar."

One of the first entries in the diary following Johnnie's indictment was dated November 9. He wrote in part (mildly edited for clarity):

November 9, 1971:

. . . Ronnie has a brother or cousin that stays on Green Lea. What's the address, I don't know. If they wanted to find anyone, they could. If they [his lawyers] wanted to find anyone [of his potential corroborating witnesses], they could. What did Sammie and his wife say?

. . . They have got Earl down here somewhere. You know I couldn't see him if I want to.

They have me locked up in a place [where] it's no one in there but me and some old mattresses and pillow and other junk and it's really cold in here.

. . . *The lady [Wilma Chestnut] that seen them won't come forward and what she seen*, so what is there for me to do but wait. I don't know anything.

. . . The paper said they indicted me on the girl's statement and a police statement. I haven't talked with no policemen, haven't anyone talked with me but the priest [Father Ralph Wright] and parole officer.

Nov. 17, 1971:

. . . I talked with Earl. I asked him why were he [sic] telling these lies on me and he said he didn't tell them. He said *Charles* is the one. If that's so, well how did Charles get out there [to Kingsbury]?

He didn't go out there when I took Ronnie out there, so who took him out there? I didn't.

. . . Earl told me that boy *Charles is in California . . . Earl had some dope on him* he said when they picked him up. I didn't even know he used dope.

. . . I can't take any more of this. *It is too much on me.* If I knew something about this I would be alright, but as it is *I don't know anything about this* and I am steady trying to figure it out.

That's why I wanted you [Wright] to see the major about getting me a lie detector test before I *do something to myself. This charge is just about to run me crazy.* If I am guilty, I will take my punishment.

I have always in the past, so if I am wrong now I will still suffer for my guilt. That's why I ask you [referring to Daisy Joiner] to get yourself someone else for *if I am guilty I know they are going to kill me* and I don't want anyone to have their mind on me.

CHAPTER 9

The Trial

By New Year's Day, the flow of donations to the Wilma Chestnut Fund was down to a trickle. No one was complaining, though. The impromptu endeavor succeeded beyond Dr. Barbour's wildest dreams.

What began as a modest proposal to offset Wilma's medical bills resulted in Sinatra paying them, leaving the fund with enough to provide Wilma with a nominal income for years. Moreover, Barbour got the Christmas miracle that he had been praying for.

A private seller who had been following news stories about the Wilma Chestnut Fund called him during the holidays and said he would sell his property in a safe and quiet neighborhood in suburban University City for only $30,000.

A real estate agent informed Barbour that homes in the neighborhood typically sold for $40,000 or more.

The news media reported that Barbour used $8,000 from the fund as a down payment, and that Colia would pay a monthly mortgage of $140 until the balance was met.

The amount of the home was less than a third of the total in the fund by the end of January. It had surpassed $100,000 – that's more than $500,000 in today's dollars.

Wilma was doing well at the Missouri School for the blind. That came as no surprise to Colia, however, because Wilma had always been a good student. She received good report cards even though she was struggling with mathematics by her freshmen year.

Hoping to get her high school diploma in two years instead of the anticipated three, Wilma was disappointed when she discovered that the school was little more than a rehabilitation hospital in an academic setting.

Founded in 1851, the school was privately funded for the first five years. By it 20th anniversary, the state-funded school housed over 100 students on its rapidly expanding campus, and a student could attend from the first grade through high school graduation.

Instead of academics, the school's main focus was on fostering mobility and teaching Braille.

A middle-aged woman facing the complete loss of her sight within several months tried enrolling at the school around the same time as Wilma.

The woman was turned away because the school informed her that training her on how to get around now would only delay and even interfere with her rate of progress once was completely blind.

The other thing that shocked Wilma happened on the first day. She thought that she would hear the incessant clatter of canes as she entered the school, only to discover that none of the students bothered using canes because they had memorized the building.

Even with some training, Wilma struggled for a long time with her fear of falling down steps.

A more pleasant surprise was Carolyn Renn, her roommate. The two girls shared similar tastes in sports, fashion, and music. They spent hours listening to soul on Wilma's new cassette player and listening to pop and rock on Carolyn's turntable.

They shared a love for the Chilites, but Wilma wasn't as big a fan of the Jackson 5 as Carolyn. The Jackson 5, Wilma argued, had too much of the popular "bubble-gum sound."

As luck would have it, Wilma ended up meeting the very group that Carolyn would have given her right arm to chat with.

Merdean Fielding, a gospel singer who covered the local music scene for the *St. Louis Argus*, had arranged to interview the Jackson 5 when they returned to St. Louis on February 12 for a concert at Kiel Auditorium.

She invited Wilma to accompany her.

The group was fronted by 13-year-old Michael. The group's PR team told reporters that he was eleven. They were at the height of their popularity. By the time they cut their third album in 1970, they had appeared on practically every entertainment show on television.

They were working on their own variety show, and they starred in a Saturday morning cartoon show featuring the group and their misadventures around the world.

When Fielding and Wilma arrived at the large suite reserved for the brothers at the Chase-Park Plaza Hotel, local radio personality and the evening's emcee Bernie Hayes was there taking photos.

Hayes enjoyed a special relationship with the group, having introduced them to the St. Louis area in 1966 when they were on the "chitlin' circuit.

Ms. Fielding was interviewing the brothers and was especially trying to get a few good quotes from Michael, the main reason for the group's skyrocket to fame.

Michael, unfortunately, experienced a delayed childhood and was making up for lost time.

As she stared in disbelief, Michael used the big bed as a trampoline while answering her questions. He had grown bored with interviews by then, but he knew that he had to go along. Behaving like a kid half his real age was how he dealt with it.

"Stop it, Michael!" the other brothers yelled. "Be still for a minute."

Michael wasn't having it. Wilma found herself lifting her head up as Michael jumped into the air, and lowering her head when he landed on the mattress.

Since she couldn't see him, it was the only way she could follow the rising and falling level of his voice.

"Michael!" Jackie yelled. "Come on, now. That's enough. We have guests. Answer the lady's questions."

Michael would stop, but the minute he started answering the next question he would start jumping up and down again. Wilma started feeling sorry for Ms. Fielding and the older brothers.

"Man, that is one hard-headed little boy," she said to herself. "Somebody needs to give him a good spanking because he's out of control."

She was joking – sort of. She knew that it must be hard on a child that young to be the center of so much attention. They were trying to make him grow up too fast, and it was showing.

Jackie asked the reporter about Wilma, who was so nervous that she sat almost perfectly still with her hands on her lap during the interview. Ms. Fielding explained what had happened to Wilma and how excited she was to be there.

Although he had just gotten out of the shower and was only wearing a robe over a pair of pants, Jackie told Wilma that he and Michael would be honored to have a photograph taken with her.

"And I would be honored to have a picture taken with you," she replied excitedly. "My roommate loves you all!"

Eager to become part of the moment, the Jackson 5's chauffeur jumped between Wilma and Michael and grabbed Wilma by the hands.

Jackie sat on the arm of the chair on which Wilma was sitting and leaned against her. It was not flirtatious; it was just his way of saying that he cared.

"I hope whoever hurt you goes to jail for a long time," he said. Before she could reply, Bernie Hayes told everyone to "say cheese" and snapped a photo.

By March, Wilma was forced to turn to serious matters. The criminal trial was only two months away, meaning that she had to try to remember as much as she could about the attack that led to the loss of her eyesight.

Neither Earl nor Johnnie could afford an attorney, so they were at the mercy of the state's nascent "public defender" system promulgated after the *Miranda* decision. A key part of the decision required the court to provide attorneys to those unable to pay for one.

Most established lawyers did not want to practice criminal law, so an indigent defendant charged with a serious crime often wound up hiring the "ambulance chasers" who hung around in the lobby of the courthouse, essentially soliciting clients (which was then illegal).

Gerald Rabushka, the man appointed to represent Earl, said that he hadn't practice criminal law because "there was no money in it unless your client was rich."

A graduate of St. Louis University's School of Law, Rabushka served as a prosecutor during a two-year stint in the Air Force after receiving his juris doctor degree in 1955. Upon leaving the military, he hung out his shingle in suburban Clayton.

Real estate law formed one-third of his practice, and personal injury cases constituted the rest.

Although he had never tried a criminal case, he was among hundreds of attorneys willing to do pro bono work to prevent the criminal court from buckling under the backlog caused by *Miranda*.

"If I recall correctly, Harper didn't even have any serious crimes on his juvenile record when he came to me," Rabushka said.

"I interviewed him a couple of times before trial and decided that there was no need for this kid to end up in the penal system. Since the prosecution had no case without his testimony, my goal was to get the best deal possible for him."

Richard C. Wuestling was appointed to represent Johnnie. He was ranked among the top litigators in Saint Louis by the early 1970s. Although he rarely accepted criminal cases, he had tried enough to battle toe-to-toe with the city's brightest attorneys.

Born in Saint Louis in 1928, he was the nephew of George "Yats" Wuestling, the colorful shortstop for the Detroit Lions for two seasons (1929-1930) and the New York Yankees for one season.

Standing over six feet tall and weighing more than 200 pounds, Wuestling was torn between playing professional football and baseball. He chose the latter after the Yankees offered the 19-year-old a $5,000 signing bonus.

It was one of the highest amounts the team had ever paid to a rookie. He spent two seasons playing for the Independence Yankees of Independence, Kansas, the minor league affiliate of the New York Yankees. At the time, rookies were routinely sent to the minor league camp for basic training.

By the end of the second year in the minors, he was disillusioned. Televisions were unavailable in most towns where the team traveled, and he was barred from reading because the manager said it would ruin his "batting" eye.

He wanted a more stationary lifestyle and something more certain than a season or two in professional sports. After getting married and earning his undergraduate degree through evening classes (a common practice at the time), Wuestling was accepted at Washington University's School of Law in St. Louis, from which he graduated in 1959.

Wuestling had to check his car every morning as the trial neared because of repeated death threats. He would sprinkle pine needles on the hood every night. If they were all gone in the morning, he assumed that someone had raised the hood and planted explosives.

City attorney Henry J. Fredericks was chosen to try the case. While he was a seasoned attorney – having prosecuted hundreds of cases in the past 15 years – it had been years since he won a highly publicized trial.

In 1958, Fredericks tried a teenager for manslaughter after three people were killed at a drag race near Riverview Drive and Chain of Rocks Bridge. It was the first case in Missouri history where the person charged did not actually kill the victims.

Robert Fennewald was racing against another teenager when their cars collided and his opponent hit another car not involved in the race. Every occupant of the third car died. Fennewald was convicted and sentenced to a year at the Missouri Penitentiary.

Fredericks also generated headlines by sending a young black man to the gas chamber at a critical juncture in the controversy over capital punishment.

After initially professing innocence, Lloyd Leo Anderson confessed to killing a delivery boy during a drug store robbery in 1961. He also admitted killing several other people during a string of 30 robberies.

Anderson said he killed the boy because he wouldn't "stop hollering."

He died in the gas chamber in February 1965 at the very moment that the state legislature was debating the constitutionality of the death penalty.

Fredericks failed in a bid, however, to unravel a murder mystery involving a dentist who performed abortions on the side.

Dr. Glennon Engleman was suspected of killing people to collect insurance benefits. His first known victim was James S. Bullock, the husband of Engleman's former wife.

Bullock was gunned down in December 1958 while walking to an evening class at St. Louis University.

Edna Ruth Bullock and Engleman took the Fifth Amendment when taken in for questioning. She collected $87,000 in insurance benefits six months after marrying Bullock. Her annual salary was only $4,500 at the time.

Engleman escaped justice until 1985, when he was sentenced to 50 years for his role in the murder of two more men killed in order to collect their insurance benefits.

No one knows how many others fell victim to the deadly dentist.

The average St. Louisan considered the case against Brooks a "slam dunk," but Fredericks knew better. Although pretrial publicity all but guaranteed a conviction, a procedural error or a surprise witness could jeopardize a sure thing. He had lost sure things before.

The public was completely unaware that Fredericks had no physical evidence against the defendants.

The most he had were photos of the apartment taken on the evening of September 23 by Patrolman Emil G. Philipak. These included an overview of the apartment and a photo showing the broken window.

From March 22, the day the media revealed that Johnnie would go on trial in 60 days, Wuestling and Rabushka wondered whether their clients would even make it to trial.

They learned from guards inside the jail that an attempt to kill Johnnie would be made as he left for court. Their offices also received dozens of threats from anonymous callers who threatened to kill Johnnie inside the courtroom itself.

Police claimed that members of several black power organizations were conspiring to have Johnnie killed before or during trial.

Fearing for his client's safety and his own, Wuestling filed a motion for extra security precautions.

Judge Palumbo granted the request to have all rear exits to the courtroom locked. Everyone entering the courtroom had to submit to a full body search.

It was, as the media noted, some of the "most elaborate security precautions in Municipal Court history."

The jury consisted of eleven men and one woman; three were black.

Officer Dampier was the first witness called on May 22, the first day of trial. His testimony was unexceptional. He merely reiterated how he found Wilma semi-nude with wounds to her eyes.

As a prosecution witness, Wilma was prevented from sitting in the courtroom while others testified. She was scheduled to take the stand on the third day of trial.

She had been preparing for months, deciding what to wear.

Determined to show her assailants that they had not derailed her life, Wilma treated herself to a manicure and pedicure the day before she was scheduled to testify.

She picked out a beautiful white dress and bought matching shoes. She wore a wig styled in the way that Diana Ross of the Supremes was wearing her hair. In short, she was dressed to impress.

Alas, it was not to be.

When Fredericks saw how attractive and prosperous Wilma looked, he realized that they had not discussed a key element of his case: courtroom presence.

"Wilma," he said, "let me say first of all that you look absolutely beautiful today."

"Thank you," she said as a few reporters looked on.

"But you know, Wilma, we don't have very much evidence against the men who hurt you, so we have to do everything we can to elicit sympathy from the jury."

"Okay," she said, "so what do you want me to do?"

"When you go into that courtroom, I want you to look as pitiful as possible," he replied. "I want you to use a cane and I want you to limp and to walk slowly."

"But," she replied, "I don't normally use a cane."

"You will today," he answered. "You have to."

As Wilma smiled incredulously, Fredericks gave her more shocking demands.

"I want you to take off your wig," he said, "and I want you to go into the bathroom and remove all of your makeup."

"While you're doing that," he continued, "I want your friend here to go home and get the raggediest pair of jeans he can find and bring them back here. I want him to bring back a shirt that's too small so the jury will think that you're too destitute to afford proper-fitting clothes."

"For real?" she asked.

"Yes. If we don't do everything in our power to win the jury's sympathy, both of the men who hurt you could get off scot-free."

There was no doubt about it. Earl's testimony against himself and Johnnie was devastating. He was called as the second witness on the first day of trial because the prosecutor wanted his account heard while the jury was still fresh.

Earl was the bread and the butter of the case against Johnnie; they knew it and the defense knew it. Unless they were able to discredit Earl, the combination of his and Wilma's testimony would all but guarantee a conviction.

Fredericks volunteered himself to demonstrate what happened to Wilma during the attack.

Earl stood up and placed his right hand on the prosecutors throat and his left hand behind his neck, forming a circle. Both Johnnie and Earl was surprised at how hard Wilma fought back.

"I put my hands over her face until she had quit jumpin'," he said.

After Wilma lost consciousness, Earl said that they lay her on the sofa and he and Earnest left with the goods.

Johnnie remained in the apartment. Earl and Earnest were shocked upon seeing him minutes later.

"He had blood on his hands," the juvenile stated when the prosecutor asked whether he noticed anything unusual about Johnnie upon his return to the getaway car. "I asked him what he did."

"You know that glass that I was drinking out of," Earl quoted Johnnie as saying.

"I broke it and stabbed her eyes out. . . . One thing about it. She won't be looking at no pictures."

The jury and the spectators released an audible gasp. Johnnie sat emotionless at the defense table.

Nearly every juror looked at Johnnie with contempt after Earl related those words.

Johnnie looked down at a writing pad on the table.

CHAPTER 10

Judgment Day

Something Earl said at the end of his testimony was a key to understanding his motive for turning against Johnnie.

By late evening on September 23, black radio stations had discovered what happened to Wilma, though it would be days before the mainstream media would pick up the story. Earl was relieved that she was alive but upset about what Johnnie did to her after he and Earnest left.

They went home after picking up Johnnie, all the time thinking that Johnnie probably killed Wilma. They spent several hours debating what to do next because Johnnie had done something that neither of them bargained for.

The broadcasts reported that Wilma's "eyes were cut out during a robbery."

Fearful of going to prison, Earl called 911. He refused to divulge his name, but he told the operator what happened. He hung up when she tried to transfer him.

Wilma took the stand on May 25. The courtroom fell silent as she entered holding on to a bailiff's arm.

"You have to take thirty-nine steps to reach the stand," he said.

Everyone focused on her. Even Johnnie looked at her briefly before turning away and pretending to read something on the pad in front of him.

After being sworn in, Wilma talked about how the defendant started flirting with her from the moment he entered the apartment.

"He asked me if I wanted another boyfriend," she said, after she told him that she already had one.

"I said, 'Nope.'"

She corroborated Earl's statement that Johnnie grabbed her around the neck, and that Earl had "put his hands over my face."

Under cross-examination by Wuestling, Wilma conceded that she did not fully regain consciousness until the day after the attack. While admitting that "Louis" was in the apartment, she said that he was not involved in the attack. The only people who harmed her were Johnnie and Earl, she said.

Colia testified the next day. She had never seen Johnnie in person, just the grainy mug shot on TV and in the newspapers. She looked straight ahead as she walked toward the witness stand. After she took the oath and sat down, she found herself staring directly at Johnnie.

"My baby! My baby!" she cried. The trauma of seeing him for the first time was too much to bear. It appeared that she was struggling for breath and was going to pass out, so a bailiff rushed to her aid.

The moment caught everyone by surprise, including the twelve people chosen to decide Johnnie's fate. The judge ordered a brief recess while Colia was helped out of the courtroom. The prosecution called another witness to give her time to recuperate.

Ronnie Clower described how he had gone job hunting with Johnnie hours before the attack, and testified that Johnnie asked him for a knife upon taking him home and heading back to Kingsbury with Earl and "Louis."

Linda Prophet, the friend who lived with Wilma and her mother, testified that Ronnie had come by the apartment looking for Wilma the day before the attack and on the morning of the attack.

Defense witness Robert Tucker testified that he saw Johnnie around noon on September 23, which was around the time he was alleged to have been at the Kingsbury apartment. His mother, Mattie Tucker Gregory, said that she saw Johnnie on the day of the attack and he did not have sideburns. (Wilma said that her attacker had sideburns.)

Samuel Edwards testified that Johnnie was at his home at least three times on the day of the attack: once around nine o'clock, again around noon, and finally around two o'clock in the afternoon. Those times just happened to coincide with the three times that Johnnie was allegedly on Kingsbury.

"What happened to Wilma shouldn't happen to the lowest animal," Fredericks said in his closing argument. He reminded them that police found glass from the broken Steak 'n Shake mug in the toilet, and that Johnnie was the only one who drank something during the visit.

Wuestling agreed that what happened was horrific, but cautioned the jury that the only evidence against Johnnie was the testimony of a codefendant who deserved to be on trial for the same crimes.

He reminded them that defense witnesses placed Johnnie elsewhere at the time of the attack, and that Earl and Earnest might have been the actual perpetrators. He also noted that Wilma had said "Ronnie, Ronnie" when Colia asked her who blinded her.

"There is no question about this being a horrible crime. However, as bad as it is, it would be a thousand times worse to send away an innocent man for this crime."

The jury was unimpressed, with many telling reporters later that his defense was "very weak."

Wuestling did come away with an insight that might prove useful on appeal, however. Some jurors were bothered by Wilma's testimony that the man who attacked her had sideburns and a scar under his lip.

Most were able to dismiss those concerns because the defense failed to provide any information showing that any of the perpetrators fit that description.

The jury reached a unanimous verdict on the first ballot. Johnnie was found guilty on all three counts in the indictment. In addition to the robbery and assault, he was charged with violating the Missouri Habitual Offenders Act.

Johnnie was caught up in a backlash against repeat offenders. The latest Uniform Crime Report, published annually by the FBI, showed that the number of forcible rapes in Missouri doubled between 1961 (with 578 reported to police) and 1971 (1,245 reported). These were only reported rapes, mind you, one of the most underreported crimes in America.

Robbery jumped from 3,637 in 1961 to 8,533 in 1971. Aggravated assault nearly tripled between 1961 (2,828) and 1971 (8,155).

Moreover, the very same judge who sent Johnnie to the penitentiary on the robbery charge was trying him again.

Paschal "P.F." Palumbo was a no-nonsense jurist who had seen too many violent offenders serve less that one-fourth of the time he had given them. A native St. Louisan, he served in the Army as a staff sergeant in World War II. After graduating from St. Louis University, he formed a small law firm and worked there until 1965, when Governor Warren E. Hearnes appointed him to the Circuit Court bench.

On December 1, 1967, Palumbo had sentenced Johnnie to eight years for first-degree robbery with a dangerous and deadly weapon. He only served two years.

When the *Globe-Democrat* railed against lenient treatment of violent offenders and named Johnnie by name, perhaps Judge Palumbo took it personally.

It wasn't his fault that Johnnie was back on the streets after only 2 years, yet the editorial implied that it was. It must have angered him that a man he ordered locked up until at least 1973 had gotten early and had committed a far worse offense.

Palumbo seemed determined to make sure that Johnnie would be too old to hurt anyone before he saw freedom again. Pending a hearing on presentencing report (which takes into account a defendant's past crimes, family background, and other factors) Palumbo sentenced him to 15 years on the robbery charge and 55 years for the aggravated assault.

Johnnie, who sat handcuffed at the defense table, lowered his head in disbelief.

Wuestling reassured him that the battle was just beginning. He filed an immediate notice of appeal.

The drama outside the courthouse was as intense as it had been inside the courtroom.

Mary Childs, Johnnie's mother, was hysterical. She portrayed Johnnie as a good son who had experienced a hard life growing up without a father.

One of nine children, Johnnie had struggled with diabetes since he was fourteen, she said. Although his health prevented him from holding a steady job, she said, Johnnie was a good mechanic who earned a living working on cars.

His oldest brother burned to death in a car fire in 1969. A sister was born with severe birth defects. His experience with his disabled sister made Johnnie sympathetic to the disabled, his mother said, which is why she felt certain that he could never hurt someone else's child.

"As long as there is breath in my body," she said, "I'm going to fight this . . . My son never had sideburns in his life. He doesn't have broad shoulders, and he doesn't have a scar."

"I know the boy they're calling Louis," she added. "He's the one who fits the description of the husky person with sideburns."

Daisy Joiner, his common law wife, agreed. She said that the fugitive Earnest fit the description of the man who attacked Wilma. She seemed most upset that Earl was the only real witness against Johnnie, and yet he wasn't standing trial after admitting to being there.

"If I'm charged with the same thing," Joiner said, "I'd try to save my neck, too."

Mrs. Childs pointed to further "evidence" of her son's innocence. Why would Johnnie blind Wilma and then contribute a hard-earned dollar to the Wilma Chestnut Fund? To her, it just did not make any sense.

"We scrimp to give him money for cigarettes and a little change," she said. "But when he did that, I told him it was better to give than to receive."

A short distance away, Colia cried, laughed, and cried again as she hugged Wilma with all her might. Confident that they were safe now that Johnnie was going away for the rest of his life, Colia told supporters that they would soon move into their new home.

Asked about her reaction to comments made by Ms. Childs, she chose diplomacy.

"Ms. Johnnie has my deepest compassion and sympathy," she said. "He is her child as Wilma is mine, and I know the feelings of a mother. We would like to forget about it, let it fade from our minds as times goes by. We want to live and plan for tomorrow."

She declined to comment when asked whether she believed Johnnie was the man who blinded Wilma. "The jury seemed to have taken everything into consideration," she replied.

Judge Palumbo certainly had. His review of Johnnie's record showed a man with a very violent past. The indictment included only the two felonies that sent Johnnie to the Missouri Penitentiary. There were other crimes for which he had not received prison time, however, and they remained on his record. Several were significant because they were similar to the attack on Wilma.

The first crime happened a year before he was arrested for assaulting Wilma, and it involved the use of a knife. With no attempt to disguise himself, Johnnie walked into the North Side YMCA building on August 20 and approached the desk clerk. After asking a few questions about membership, he pulled out a sharp knife and demanded the clerk's money and wristwatch.

William Carpenter, the clerk, watched as Johnnie ran from the building. He grabbed a gun from his duffle bag and ran outside, where he spotted Johnnie getting into a truck. He fired several shots as Johnnie sped off.

A police officer in the vicinity heard the gunfire and headed toward the sound. He saw Carpenter standing outside with the warm gun in his hand. After Carpenter put the gun down and put his hands up, he told the officer what happened. The officer took the gun and told Carpenter to go back inside the building until he returned.

He jumped into his squad car and followed the truck. He found it parked a few blocks away and found Johnnie in a nearby tavern. After placing him under arrest, he found the watch and five of the ten dollars taken from Carpenter in Johnnie's pocket.

The charges were dismissed, however, because Carpenter didn't want to prosecute. Each time that Johnnie was released from prison, he was arrested for rape and sodomy within a year. He avoided prosecution only because the victims in both cases refused to testify against him.

Rape trials were barbaric in the 1960s. The victim was usually portrayed as a harlot who was "just asking for it." Defense attorneys would demand a list of every man the victim had ever dated or slept with, and would then use that information to suggest that the victim consented.

That's why rape was the least reported of all felonies.

In fact, a woman raped by Johnnie was in Homer G. at the same time as Wilma. She told police that Johnnie broke into her apartment, orally sodomized her and then rammed the top part of a broomstick into her vagina.

Although she told police about the incident, she did not want to be subjected to the humiliation of a trial since it was her word against his.

In many ways, then, Wilma was glad to have police protection during the trial. She and Colia were under 24-hour police protection from May 20 until the trial was over.

Judgment Day

Three days after the verdict, Fredericks dismissed the felony charges against Earl. He reduced the assault charge to a misdemeanor. As part of his guilty plea, Earl received a one-year suspended sentence and was placed on probation.

The press ignored the case, but Johnnie's supporters saw this as further proof that he had been framed.

After moving into their new home on June 1, Wilma started working part-time at Carondelet Savings & Loan Association.

The St. Louis Union Trust Company would manage the more than $95,000 remaining after the down payment on the house. It had to be completely furnished, however, since thieves had stolen everything in the vacated apartment on Newstead.

On August 5, Johnnie stood before Circuit Court Judge Pascal F. Palumbo to hear his fate. Judge Palumbo asked him if he had anything to say before the he ruled. The jury had already recommended a 55-year term for Johnnie, but Judge Palumbo had the authority to lessen or increase it.

"You are sentencing me for something I didn't do and don't know anything about," Johnnie protested. "If you are going to take my life from me, take it right away. What you are doing now is wrong. You know it and I know it."

"As you can see," Johnnie said as he removed his coat from his shoulders, "I am not broad-shouldered. I've never been husky."

He recapped Wilma's testimony about her attacker having sideburns. "I'm unable to grow sideburns," he argued.

After Johnnie finished his plea, Palumbo told Johnnie that he was denying the motion for a new trial, and that he would confirm the jury's sentence with one alteration. He ruled that the two sentences would run concurrently rather than consecutively.

Johnnie broke into tears as Palumbo said: "You are hereby sentenced to a term of 55 years" in state prison. His mother and wife Daisy cried out as bailiffs led him out of the courtroom.

The nightmare that Johnnie feared engulfed him even before he entered prison. His sentencing made local news headlines, and inmates in a local jail were anxious to exact their own punishment on him were on alert.

For the next two weeks, Johnnie was a man who slept on his back with one eye open. Finally, Johnnie was informed that on August 16 he was being transferred to the Missouri State Penitentiary in Jefferson City.

Shortly before noon, an officer went to Johnnie's cell and told him to pack his things because his transfer was imminent.

At 12:15, a deputy went to the cell to remove him. He found Johnnie holding a razor against his throat.

"I ain't goin' nowhere!" he shouted.

"And if you try to make me, I'll kill myself."

The deputy left the holding area and called the warden. Around half past noon, the warden and the deputy returned to Johnnie's cell. As the warden unlocked the door, Johnnie ran the razor across the right side of his neck.

Blood dripped from the cut as the deputy wrestled Johnnie to the floor, forced the razor from his hand, and handcuffed him. The warden issued a call for an ambulance. It arrived in a matter of minutes and rushed Johnnie to Homer G. Phillips Hospital.

The cut, as it turned out, was only superficial; it delayed Johnnie's date with the penitentiary by less than three hours. At three o'clock, emergency room physicians notified the warden that Johnnie would not be admitted.

The cut was on the side of his neck, they noted, and had been patched up with only four or five stitches. An hour later, Johnnie was on his way to the penitentiary.

Fully aware of the threats from inmates to kill him upon his arrival, the bandaged Johnnie immediately requested placement in a maximum security cell, which was granted.

"We can't keep him like this for 55 years, Warden Harold Swenson told reporters. "But we'll keep him there pending the outcome of his appeal."

A subsequent investigation of how Johnnie obtained the razor was conducted. All of the razors that inmates had been given on the morning Johnnie cut himself were accounted for, the warden claimed.

He told reporters that because there was a very strict accounting process for razors, someone must have smuggled one into the jail for Johnnie.

"That happens no matter what we do. We do everything we can to stop it but they still get in. We even find hacksaw blades smuggled in sometimes."

A small group of loyal supporters argued that the suicide attempt proved that Johnnie was innocent.

"He repeatedly told us that he was innocent during the months we prepared for trial," defense lawyer Wayne Wright said. "He said that he would rather commit suicide than go up for a bum rap."

Wuestling also maintained his client's innocence. "He was been in trouble before," he told reporters. "Those times, he always confessed to the police. This time, he insisted that he was innocent."

Mary Childs, Johnnie' mother, remained convinced that Earnest and Harper had framed her son.

To prove to police that he had not blinded Wilma, Ms. Childs took the clothing that he had allegedly worn on the day of the crime to the police station and asked them to examine them for evidence of blood or signs of a struggle.

"They refused to even look at the clothes," she said. "The whole case was a frame-up. It isn't over yet," she warned.

The last witness who came to Johnnie' defense was Father Wright, the Benedictine monk who had first approached Johnnie in October 1971. Wright told reporters that Johnnie had written a detailed statement of his activities on the day of the blinding.

"I visited him weekly and tried to check the facts for him," Wright said. "I am convinced he is not the man who slashed her eyes. I was able to verify what he told me."

Wright added that he had visited people who said they had seen Johnnie on the day of the crime. But when asked to explain what evidence he had to support Johnnie' claim of innocence, Wright refused.

"I am not going to say anything about what I know, but I'm not going to sit back and do nothing."

CHAPTER 11

Monk

What happened to Johnnie at the hospital was almost unimaginable. A nurse who had befriended Wilma called and gave her all the details.

No one in the emergency room wanted to touch him, literally.

Johnnie pressed a gauze pad against his neck while a nurse roamed the hospital seeking an intern willing to help him. A foreign intern finally agreed to stitch up the wound. It took him less than ten minutes.

"The intern told a nurse to bandage Johnnie's neck and then hand him over to the sheriff," she recalled, "but no one wanted to touch him."

"So a nurse took a large bandage out of a box and threw it at Johnnie and told him to put it on his own damn neck."

They were only toying with him in a way, since they all knew that there would be serious repercussions if word leaked out about how they had treated him. A nurse finally took clean gauze and taped it over the wound.

Some of them clapped as Johnnie was led away, relieved that he would not be admitted. A few were the very same people on duty the afternoon that Wilma had come in bleeding from both eyes.

Johnnie's supporters, particularly his mother and Father Wright, were furious about how casually law enforcement officials regarded his suicide attempt. Johnnie also told his mother about how he was treated at the hospital.

"His wounds were not being treated properly," Ms. Childs said. "Guards and inmates at the prison have already threatened to kill him."

In the meantime, Wilma settled into her new home, comfortable with the knowledge that Johnnie would never be free to hurt anyone else.

As soon as Johnnie gave his court appointed attorney's name to Father Wright, the monk went on a crusade to prove that Johnnie was innocent.

He gave him copies of all the information he had gathered since Johnnie's arrest. Some of it was useful – the names, phone numbers and addresses of people whom Johnnie claimed would testify that he was at home or with them at the time of the assault.

Some of it was pure speculation. In fact, Wright gave his weekly summaries of his theories such titles as "Speculation of August 12, 1972" and subtitles such as "Growth Toward Conviction" and "Truthtelling."

According to the monk, here's what really happened:

Johnnie picked up Ronnie Clower around six o'clock on the morning of September 23. They drove to the auto assembly plant in Fenton and filled out employment applications.

Ronnie told him to stop by his girlfriend's best friend's house on the way back because he wanted to introduce them (even though Wilma had a boyfriend and Johnnie was in a common law marriage).

They stopped by Wilma's house, but "Wilma's sister" (actually it was Linda Prophet) told them that Wilma was babysitting on Kingsbury.

On the way there they saw Earl, one of Johnnie's neighbors who had just left school after his "free period" at Beaumont High School.

Earl hopped into the 1962 Cadillac and the three went to see Wilma.

The visit lasted about twenty minutes, during which Johnnie requested two or three glasses of water. On the way back to Ronnie's house, they saw a guy nicknamed Scar (Earnest Craine), whom Earl knew.

Since Johnnie recognized him, they offered Scar a lift to his sister's house. As Johnnie was dropping off Ronnie, Scar asked Johnnie if he had a knife in his possession. Johnnie said no.

Scar asked Ronnie the same question, so Ronnie ran inside and got one for him.

Scar and Earl exited the car and started walking, but Johnnie didn't know where they were headed. It was about nine o'clock (which suggested that Earl's free period must have been the first period of the day).

As soon as he dropped them off, he went to Tate's Garage, where he "met up" with his cousin Sammie Edwards. They worked on Sammie's car for some time. Johnnie never returned to Kingsbury, and he never saw Ronnie, Earl or Scar again that day.

An investigator working with the monk found witnesses who said that Ronnie had a notorious reputation in his neighborhood (a few blocks from Wilma's house).

Wright concluded that Wilma was either too afraid to implicate Ronnie, or that she was persuaded not to implicate Ronnie after pleadings from Laura, her best friend and Ronnie's girlfriend.

Evangelist Barbara Drury visited Wilma the day after the attack, the monk wrote, and could confirm that Wilma said "Ronnie did it" when asked who blinded her.

Laura must have visited Wilma some time later and persuaded her not to tell anyone else that Ronnie was the culprit. Since Wilma believed that either Scar or Johnnie blinded her, she agreed not to implicate Ronnie in the crimes.

Maybe she agreed because Ronnie threatened to harm her if she implicated him, Wright suggested.

Once the agreement was struck with Laura, he surmised, Wilma decided to tell police that Earl, Johnnie and Scar were the assailants. They were the ones who drove back to Kingsbury.

Wilma gave false testimony against Johnnie in order to protect Ronnie. The proof that she committed perjury was her identification testimony. It clearly showed that she was confusing Johnnie with Scar.

It was also possible, he conceded, that the mistaken identity was unintentional.

"It's very likely that she confused the two (Louis and Johnnie) in her mind," he wrote seven days after Johnnie was formally sentenced.

Scar bragged about blinding Wilma, he claimed, then decided to leave town. Left to face the charges alone, Ronnie got angry and "threatened Earl."

Fearful, the juvenile agreed with Ronnie's plan to blame the whole thing on Johnnie.

Wilma made one big mistake, the monk wrote.

She told Drury that Ronnie, Earl and Scar were the three who came back a second time. Now all Drury had to do was get Wilma on tape making the same statement.

Wright was relentless in his pursuit of justice for Johnnie. He had visited Johnnie weekly since early October 1971 and was firmly convinced that he was framed.

Johnnie's sister told him in late October that there was a rumor that Scar was the one who blinded Wilma, and that was the reason he left town so quickly.

In January 1972, a friend of the monk paid for a private investigator to interview the people whom Johnnie claimed could verify his whereabouts from September 22 through his alleged hospitalization on September 23.

Charles Willis reported back after a few days of canvassing and said Johnnie's story checked out. He cautioned Wright that while many of the witnesses confirmed Johnnie's story, some made it plain that there was no way that they would testify on his behalf.

With all the negative publicity surrounding the case, a few people said that they were afraid of being fired or physically attacked if it became known that they were "backing Johnnie."

Wright used his own money to pay for a copy of Wilma's deposition from February 23 and Earl's deposition of April 6.

He noted that Wilma had described Johnnie as having "flaring out sideburns" and a "funny looking lip." He jotted down this note next to Wilma's description: "Brooks cannot grow sideburns and his lip is normal."

But Wilma's words were not quite that specific.

––––––––––––––

Question: Was there anything about Johnnie's face that attracted your attention?

WILMA: I wasn't paying too much attention to him, but I think he had a scar or something . . . *I don't know.*

———————

It was only after repeated questioning that Wilma started to confuse Johnnie's features with those of the man who called himself Louis that day.

The discrepancy might be useful at the trial, Wright and Wuestling agreed, but Wuestling knew he would have to be gentle with his cross-examination of Wilma.

Wilma was about five feet and five inches tall and only weighed about 110 pounds.

Since he had the physique of an NFL linebacker, Wuestling was sharp enough to recognize that ripping apart a fragile blind girl would cause the jury to convict Johnnie out of sympathy alone.

He had trouble getting Wright to accept this. The monk wanted to take the witness stand. He wanted the jury to read the 3,000-word statement that Johnnie wrote to him.

Wright visited Earl in jail on April 8. According to the monk's notes, Earl said that he didn't know who blinded Wilma.

Wilma and her cousin knew exactly what happened, Earl allegedly told him. He refused to identify the cousin, Wright noted.

"Tell Brooks I'm gonna get out of this any way I can," Earl said as Wright prepared to leave.

"They'll never catch Scar [because] he won't be back until this case is over. There are four people involved in this thing whose names I haven't given even to my lawyer because I don't want to get them involved."

A few days later, the monk notified Mrs. Childs of his findings, particularly Wilma's testimony about "Johnnie" having flaring out sideburns and the scar on his lip.

The information hit her hard because she had seen Scar a number of times and knew that those were his features. She is convinced now more than ever that her son is being framed.

In a follow-up visit on May 6, the monk wrote that Earl confirmed Johnnie's statement that they all arrived at the Kingsbury apartment around nine thirty on September 23.

He observed that the time corroborated Johnnie's statement, but conflicted with statements by Ronnie and Wilma that they arrived for the first time around noon.

Wuestling told Wright that statements made by Earl in the deposition gave the impression that the youth was "congenital liar . . . stories spume forth and contradict one another."

Johnnie's conviction did nothing to slow down the monk's crusade.

A detective working on Johnnie's behalf told the monk that police withheld a report taken at the hospital in which Wilma specifically named Ronnie as the person who attacked her.

Wright noted that an eyewitness named John Philips overheard Wilma's statement about Ronnie and later called the police to report it.

In September 1972, the monk jotted in his newsletter that Drury "befriended Wilma one day after the incident."

Drury told him that Wilma accused Ronnie of the crime. Wilma also confessed that the man who blinded her "had a scar."

Wright obtained a copy of a June 1971 arrest record for Earnest Charles Craine (aka Louis, Scar) from a detective. He noted that this was three months before Wilma was blinded, so the mug shot would be an accurate representation of how Scar looked in September.

The mug shot, he noted, "showed the beginnings of flaring out kind of sideburns."

Because the photo is so grainy, the monk invited the detectives and another investigator over to the lab room at St. Abbey's school. After placing the mug shot under a microscope, they agreed that there was a scar beneath Craine's lower lip.

Armed with more than 140 "letters" from Johnnie (many of them less than one page), Earl's statements to the monk, depositions of both Earl and Wilma, and the trial transcript, Johnnie's defense team began writing their brief for the Missouri Court of Appeals.

In the meantime, Wilma tried to put the case behind her.

Unhappy with the curriculum at the Missouri School for the Blind, Wilma withdrew in November 1972 and enrolled in an alternative high school.

She met a 17-year-old girl who was attending the school after having dropped out of public school when she became pregnant in her freshman year.

Tonya Freeman was having trouble with her mother and told Wilma that she was looking for a place to stay. Since Wilma had plenty of room in her new home, she invited Tonya to move in with her family.

She was the first of many people in need who would turn to Wilma for assistance. Tonya had heard about Wilma from the newspapers, of course, but she also knew a great deal about the man convicted of blinding her.

Her mother was close friend of evangelist Barbara Drury. Her mother was also among a host of others would visit the Missouri Penitentiary in Jefferson City with Drury about once a week to "minister" to the male population there.

"My mother thinks that Johnnie Brooks is innocent," Tonya said one day out of the clear blue sky. The comment bothered Wilma, but she tried not to let on.

"Well, Tonya, everyone is entitled to their opinion."

Wilma told Colia about the comment, however, and it made her nervous. She told Tonya that she would have to move out since her mother visited Johnnie regularly because she was afraid that Johnnie would discover where the family lived. Tonya moved about week later.

A few days later, Wilma came to the aid of another young girl who needed shelter.

She offered her the room that Tonya had vacated. Wilma and Colia did not have time to clean the room thoroughly after Tonya moved out, so Deborah volunteered to help Wilma clean up.

As they lifted mattress to flip it over, Deborah saw a letter. Wilma asked her to pick it up and find out to whom it belonged.

"It's addressed to Tonya," Deborah said.

"It came from somebody named Johnnie Lee Brooks at the Missouri Penitentiary."

Wilma dropped the mattress and began to tremble because her mother was right. With Scar still on the loose, every precaution that the family had taken to keep their location a secret was for naught.

Johnnie made it clear that he knew whose house Tonya was living in. He wrote that he could only send her three dollars for the time being, but promised to send more soon.

On February 8, 1973, Drury contacted the monk with startling information. She had just gotten off the phone with Wilma and that Wilma had confirmed what the monk had long suspected.

"I have something to tell you that I won't tell anyone else," Drury quoted Wilma as saying.

"The three who came back were Ronnie, Earl and Johnnie Brooks." She added that Johnnie had a scar on his lip.

When Drury asked Wilma whether the scar was on Johnnie's face or his lip, Wilma was adamant that "it was on his lip."

Wilma also told her, Drury said, that one of the men who had come by earlier that day did not return at the time of the attack.

Since Wilma had clearly confused Scar with Johnnie, the implication was clear: Scar was the person Wilma was identifying as Johnnie, meaning that Johnnie had told the truth all along.

He had not returned to the Kingsbury apartment.

With cooperation from George Curry, a black reporter for the *St. Louis Post-Dispatch*, Father Wright devised a scheme to secretly tape a conversation between Wilma and Barbara Drury.

He hoped to get Wilma to repeat what she had allegedly told Drury about the "real Johnnie" not being involved in maiming her.

Curry took an inexpensive suction-cup type device used for taping phone conversations over to Drury's house. One end of the device plugged into the microphone jack of the recorder and the suction cup was attached on the back of the part of the phone held up to the ear.

Despite the humming, you could get a decent recording by placing the cup in the right place.

As a trained journalist, Curry must have known that taping the conversation without express consent was a possible violation of both state and federal laws.

Title III of the Omnibus Crime Control and Safe Streets Act of 1968 included civil and criminal penalties for taping without the knowledge of the party being taped.

While some states require both parties to consent, others require only the consent of one party.

Every cub reporter learned that it is illegal to eavesdrop or record a conversation between other people. The law specifically stated that if the third person could not "naturally overhear" the conversation, his participation is illegal.

Since Curry was the party who brought over the wiretapping device, his actions exposed both him and Drury to possible criminal prosecution. As Father Wright was the mastermind, it also meant that he could be prosecuted as well.

The monk's journal reveals that the surreptitious recording was made on February 21, 1973.

"Attempt to get George Curry (*Post-Dispatch* reporter convinced of Brooks [sic] innocence) to be with Barbara Drury and to record Wilma confirming the above statements [about Johnnie not being involved] eventually comes off," he wrote.

But the fifteen-minute recording lacked the bombshell that he had hoped for.

When Drury asked Wilma who came back to the apartment a second time, Wilma said that everyone returned except Ronnie.

While Wright was elated that the tape proved that Wilma had confused Johnnie with Scar, he was disappointed that Wilma did not corroborate what Drury claimed about Ronnie's participation.

Wilma had an uneasy feeling about the conversation because Drury seemed to be attempting to coax certain statements from her. She kept going back to the same questions.

Wilma decided to end the conversation.

"May I tape you," Drury asked as soon as Wilma threatened to hang up.

"No," Wilma replied. "Why do you want to tape me?"

"Oh, no reason," she replied.

Wilma hung up.

"Mrs. Drury kept the tape," the monk noted. "George Curry transcribed the text."

They say that good intentions pave the path to Hell. Producing the tape or the text for the defense team could prove the wisdom of that warning.

CHAPTER 12

The Wrong Man

Wilma's faulty description of Johnnie and Drury's claim that Wilma had confided a deep dark secret convinced Curry that the wrong man had been convicted.

He visited Johnnie on April 11. The interview ran in the evening edition of the *Post-Dispatch*. It was a sympathetic account, as it focused almost exclusively on people who believed that Johnnie was railroaded.

"I did not blind Wilma Chestnut," Johnnie stated. "One day people will see that I am innocent."

Curry pointed out how Johnnie was different from so many other prisoners who professed innocence. Johnnie was supported by a respected priest, he noted, and another unusual character witness: his former parole officer.

They believed that Johnnie suffered a miscarriage of justice, and they were not alone, Curry wrote.

Other "members of the legal community" believed that Johnnie was denied a fair trial, the article claimed, but it failed to mention anyone from that community.

The article parroted some of the comments that Johnnie had written in his 3,000 word essay to Father Wright. Brooks had always admitted when he had done wrong is the past, the article stated.

"The young lady (Wilma) testified that the person who committed this crime had broad shoulders," Brooks said.

"As you can see, mine are slender." The article failed to note that Johnnie had lost quite a few pounds on the prison diet. It also mischaracterized her testimony.

Wilma said that the man named Johnnie had his shirt open, so it *appeared* that he had broad shoulders.

"She said that the person who attacked her had long sideburns that flared out at the bottom. I've never been able to grow sideburns in my life."

"The court," he told the reporter, "has convicted the wrong man."

Indeed, Curry's story read like a recap of Alfred Hitchcock's 1956 masterpiece, "The Wrong Man," which was based on a true story.

Starring Henry Fonda as Christopher Balestrero, the story involves a man charged with a robbery committed by someone else. Circumstantial evidence and faulty eyewitness testimony doom the defendant until a juror's error leads to a mistrial.

The movie was a classic by 1973, and received considerable airplay on programs such as the "Late Show" and the "Late, Late Show" in the Sedalia - Jefferson City area, site of the state penitentiary.

Incidentally perhaps, KMOS-TV aired "The Wrong Man" about three weeks before Curry's interview with Johnnie.

The CBS affiliate featured the movie as its Friday night special. It was undoubtedly a big deal at the Missouri Penitentiary at a time when TV was the only viewing option.

Curry cited more anonymous sources who believed that Wilma's testimony "described not Brooks but Ernest [sic] Charles Craine, whom authorities sought unsuccessfully for the Chestnut crime."

While it was true that Earnest was being sought, police never had any doubt that Johnnie blinded Wilma, as the one prosecutor quoted by Curry indicated.

Curry then posed a number of questions that Johnnie wanted answered.

It was a clever way of raising issues before the public that the appeals court would get the week after Curry's article ran.

"Who really blinded Wilma Chestnut? Why did a friend, Earl Harper, lie about him? Whatever became of Ernest Charles Craine? How can he convince the public and courts that he is innocent?"

After suggesting that Earnest was the perpetrator, Curry notes that prosecutors struck a deal with Earl less than a week after Johnnie was sentenced.

Curry noted that the three lawyers working on Johnnie's defense had only tried a single criminal case among them.

"I told my lawyers I wanted to testify," Johnnie said, but they refused to let him.

"When the trial was over, people had told all those lies on me and I was sitting there looking like a fool."

"I've never hit anybody with anything but my hands," he told Curry, who noted that tears had welled in Johnnie's eyes.

"Now they're saying that I hurt this little girl. I have a 20-year-old sister who has never walked. I have more compassion than to do something like this."

It was a convincing argument unless one knew of Johnnie's past. Curry's article was essentially and opinion piece masquerading as objective journalism. He didn't challenge any of Johnnie's misstatements.

Six days later, Johnnie's lawyers filed a brief with the Missouri Court of Appeals.

They claimed that police had suppressed reports which contradicted the trial testimony of Wilma and Ronnie Clower, and that it failed to release a mug shot Earnest Charles "Scar" Craine, who fit the description of the man that Wilma accused of attacking her.

Lastly, it accused the prosecution of cutting a sweetheart deal with Earl without advising defense attorneys, who could have used that information to impeach the juvenile's testimony.

Johnnie's lawyers argued his case on the eve of his birthday, October 4. They focused on their strongest argument, the deal with Earl. One of the judges made an observation which telegraphed to both sides that the case would likely be reversed.

"The state couldn't make its case without Harper," Judge Gerald M. Smith said.

Wayne Wright, one of three defense attorneys who represented Johnnie at trial, had the chutzpah to contend that Johnnie was denied effective assistance of counsel because the other two attorneys had never argued a criminal case. The argument was never raised prior to or during the trial.

"We were overwhelmed by the enormity," he said.

Wilma and Colia tried to avoid focusing on the appeal. The idea of Johnnie being set free was unthinkable. They felt confident that the trial court decision would be upheld.

Behind the scenes, Barbara Drury kept in contact with Wilma, never letting on that she was working to get Johnnie released.

It was prom time at the Missouri School for the Blind. Wilma and her roommate Carolyn Renn got into a giggly discussion about who was going with whom. The name of this boy named Michael came up, but Carolyn said that rumor was that he did not like girls.

"Oh, that's silly," Wilma replied. "People shouldn't start rumors like that," remembering some of the cruel things that had been said to her and about her at Beaumont High.

Bullying from girls who were gang members had made attending school unbearable, which is why she dropped and settled on getting a General Equivalency Diploma (GED).

Wilma sat down and talked to Michael, who said that he really wanted to go but no one would go with him.

"I'll be your date," Wilma said.

Michael was suddenly on Cloud Nine. He couldn't believe that he finally had a date.

When Wilma mentioned this to Carolyn, she joked that perhaps Wilma could fix her up with someone, too.

After some thought, Wilma told her that she knew this lady named Barbara Drury whose son was about their age. She promised to call Jim and ask him. When she did, he agreed without hesitation.

On the night of the prom, Jim and Carolyn were inseparable. They had been talking on the telephone in recent days and had discovered that they had many interests in common.

As the two couples sat at the dinner table, the conversation turned into a discussion about parents. Each person gave a brief synopsis of his or her mother and father.

"I never met my father," Wilma said, "and you already know about my mother. She's a nurse's aide at Normandy."

When it was Jim's turn, he wouldn't reveal what his parents did for a living. Instead, he gave a description that was completely unexpected.

"My dad's a drunk and my mother is cr—"

"His mother is an evangelist who heals people over the telephone," Wilma interjected.

There was an awkward silence. Carolyn changed the subject to the latest hit music and the four talked about the choices of music being played by the deejay.

On December 27, the Court of Appeals issued a decision reversing Johnnie's conviction and remanding the case for retrial.

The three-judge panel made it clear that they were appalled by the crime, calling it a "vicious, detestable and unprovoked blinding of a seventeen year old girl."

Since the state had won the trial, the court was bound to view the facts "in the light most favorable" to prosecutors.

As such, it accepted the prosecution's argument that both Johnnie and Earnest (whose name is misspelled as Crain in the opinion) were present during the first visit, and that Johnnie was directly involved in the crimes.

It dismissed most of Johnnie's eight claims of reversible error, but held that two of the errors constituted denial of a fair trial.

Ruling that there was ample corroboration to support Johnnie's conviction for robbery, the court agreed with his lawyers that the only testimony and evidence linking Johnnie to the blinding came from Earl Harper.

The court was disturbed that Gerald Rabushka, Earl's attorney, had discussed the juvenile's "situation" with Fredericks, the special prosecutor handling the case, on the same day that Earl "retained" Rabushka.

Rabushka had testified during a deposition that if Earl became a witness for the state, all charges against him would be dropped right before he took the witness stand.

After Earl testified, Rabushka said, the prosecutor would process Earl on a minor theft charge to which Earl would have to plead guilty. In exchange, Earl would receive probation. That way, it would appear on the record that nothing improper occurred.

Fredericks denied Rabushka's account. Nonetheless, the record showed that Earl was added to the official list of prosecution witnesses the day after the meeting between the two attorneys.

Rabushka and Fredericks had a second meeting on April 6, the day that Earl was deposed by Johnnie's defense team. Before Earl testified, they secretly agreed that the deal of January 10 was good.

Rabushka said that he withheld information about the agreement from Earl, but admitted telling Earl's mother and stepfather on several occasions about the deal dismissing all felony charges against Earl.

During the deposition, Earl denied that a deal had been struck in exchange for his testimony, and neither Fredericks nor Rabushka volunteered the information to the defense team.

The court noted that the charges against Earl were dismissed on May 31, just five days after Johnnie was convicted. Finding evidence of impropriety, the court ruled that Johnnie had been denied due process.

It also ruled that Palumbo failed to give the jury proposed instructions regarding the testimony of accomplices. Citing precedent, the court held that "where an accomplice instruction is requested and the facts warrant giving it, the refusal to do so is reversible error."

But the last lines of the opinion, written by Judge Smith, were the ones that many jurists felt were a personal attack on the prosecutors.

"When those facts have been suppressed by the State, the defendant has received an inquisition, not a trial."

Wilma was out of town when the reversal was handed down. She was on winter break from classes at Forest Park Community College, so she went to New Orleans, her third trip there since the spring.

The seeds that John Pankins of the Monte Carlos had planted in Wilma's mind about her father left her with a yearning to meet him. She was curious to know if her real father was as nice as her father figure was.

When she told Colia that she wanted to meet him, she called Willis Woolridge, her father's brother, to make arrangements for Wilma to come to New Orleans.

Although Colia and Curtis Willie Woolridge got along, he had remarried years ago, so she didn't want to call him directly for fear of creating problems. Besides, Wilma wanted to surprise him.

She was Wilma Woolridge until her mother married in 1963. Her father had three more daughters: 20-year-old Joyce, 15-year-old Willette, and 12-year-old Sheila.

It was a modest brood compared to his brother Willis, the father of two boys and 14 daughters.

Wilma and her step sister Ernestine hopped on a Greyhound Bus for New Orleans on March 3 for a five-day visit, which included Fat Tuesday, of course.

Uncle Willis picked them up and took them to a billiards hall near Mazant Street where her father lived. He was leaning over the table preparing for a shot as they entered.

He stopped in mid-shot as the door opened, however, as though he sensed her presence. His eyes lit up the moment her saw her, Willis told her later. Willis, who made the formal introduction, escorted Wilma to him.

Her father was very quiet. After a few seconds, Wilma broke the ice.

"I don't get a hug or a handshake or anything?" she said smiling.

"Oh, my God . . . I can't believe you're here . . . I'm just so surprised to see you. You look just like your aunt."

Curtis shook Wilma's hand as everyone in the pool hall stared. Wilma released his hand and hugged him.

Word about the stranger's background traveled quickly as they embraced, and all you could see were these tough grown men trying to hide their tears.

"Welcome home, Wilma!" some shouted.

"Welcome to Mardi Gras!"

Meeting the rest of the family was bittersweet. Willette had been diagnosed with ovarian cancer about a year earlier and was very ill.

Wilma sensed good vibrations from her father's wife; they bonded instantly.

Curtis and Willis were both members of the Zulu Social Aid and Pleasure Club, one of the largest organizations in New Orleans. They were an integral part of Fat Tuesday.

Wilma soon discovered that she could do anything she desired during the festival.

Moments after she requested permission to ride on a motorcycle during a parade, she was on the back of a Harley-Davidson. Thirty minutes later she was riding horseback with one of her father's friends who was an officer in the Zulus.

The party lasted from Saturday night through Fat Tuesday, and Wilma was sad to go.

In July, she returned to New Orleans. The visit was a somber one, as Willette had lost her battle with cancer. Even though Wilma had only known her sister briefly, she felt the loss as much as everyone else.

Wilma enjoyed being with her father so much that spending time with him was all she could think about when she wasn't doing homework or working at her part-time job.

He asked her to come back in December so they could spend their first Christmas together. That's why reporters were unable to reach her when the appeals court threw out Johnnie's conviction.

She didn't return to St. Louis until December 30. She wanted to celebrate New Year's Eve with her boyfriend.

Reporters finally caught up with her about a week later. If they anticipated finding a girl depressed at the thought of having to go through a trial again, they were disappointed.

Wilma was so busy living her life that she hadn't spent much time dwelling on the past. In fact, she was preparing to enter the Miss Black St. Louis beauty pageant from the moment she came home.

They wanted to know how she felt about the court decision, and whether she had forgiven Johnnie for blinding her.

"I wouldn't say that I've forgiven him," she answered. "I just don't have any bitterness toward him. Of course, if he were released from prison, it would always be on my mind that he's out there."

She also surprised them with her optimism about life without vision. "My flexibility really helps," she said. "I can groove in any situation."

"Really," she added, "the only two things that have bothered me were coming to steps and having to go down them, and having someone stand next to me and not say anything."

Colia declined repeated requests to comment on the appellate court's decision. So did Dr. Barbour and prosecutors.

Mary Childs, Johnnie's mother, also refused comment.

The only person willing to speak publicly was Father Wright. His investigation had guided the defense's case from the start, and victory was now in hand.

"A lot of things will come out" in the retrial to support Johnnie's innocence, he promised reporters. "There were so many individual factors indicating that Brooks was wrongly accused."

Wilma had accomplished much since the last time reporters encircled her. She left the Missouri School for the Blind to obtain her GED. She stayed long enough to learn how to function in a world without vision, but that was about all the school could offer her.

After earning her GED, she enrolled at Forest Park Community College, where she earned high marks in her first semester.

A rabid fan of "Longstreet," Wilma started taking karate classes with her boyfriend. She also pursued her interest in art, focusing on sculpture, pottery, and sewing.

In mid-January, she entered the Miss Black St. Louis pageant.

Although Wilma and Colia refused to let Johnnie's victory distract them, the editorial writers at the *St. Louis Globe-Democrat* were livid. It condemned the appeals court decision, calling it "an excuse to assist the defendant, rather than protect to public interest."

"The whole weight of the Appeals Court's order of reversal is on an unfounded assumption that the jury might not have believed Harper if the jurors thought Harper had been offered a deal."

The final salvo was at the *Post-Dispatch*, its chief competitor, for its "biased" coverage.

"While in prison, Brooks has had the benefit of public sympathy created by newspaper stories prompted by persons who believe him to be inno-cent. . . No evidence that would tend to exonerate Brooks has been made public."

Reacting to Johnnie's claim that pretrial publicity denied him a fair trial, the editorial stated that pretrial coverage paled in comparison to "the number of sob sister stories since his conviction, aimed at opening the prison doors for him to re-enter society."

State prosecutors filed papers on January 11 asking the appellate court to reconsider its decision to overturn Johnnie's conviction.

Just as the editorial the day before had done, prosecutors suggested that Judge Smith had bent the law in Johnnie's favor, and asked for a rehearing en banc – meaning one before the full court instead of only three judges.

Smith's attack on Fredericks was labeled inappropriate and indicated that the state did not get a fair review from him for that very reason.

It also argued that the appeals court was forcing prosecutors to engage in disclosure processes far beyond anything required by recent Supreme Court decisions.

The motion was denied three months later. It ordered prosecutors to give Johnnie a new trial.

Wilma works with instructors at the Missouri School of the Blind to relearn things most take for granted: how to apply makeup; how to walk down a corridor; and decorating a Christmas tree.

Photo courtesy of Bernie Hayes

Wilma poses with Michael and Jackie Jackson (and their chauffeur) in a downtown hotel room just before a sold-out Jackson 5 concert in St. Louis. (1972)

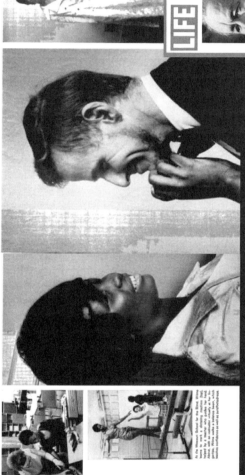

PARTING SHOTS

A brave girl makes a home in a world of touch and sound

BY BETTY DUNN

AUGUST 1914

A vivid battle scene from the Nobel Prize winner's new novel of World War I

ALEXANDER SOLZHENITSYN

LIFE magazine featured Wilma in its June 1972 issue. The article included several photos from the Wilma Chestnut Ball, an event that raised over $10,000 for her rehabilitation.

SCAR ON LIP OF
ERNEST CHARLES CRAINE (LOUIS, SCAR)

Extract from Resume of the Deposition of Wilma Chestnut
Taken on February 23 1972

None of the men had identifying scars although she believed that Johnnie's
lip looked a little funny. (p.2, 3rd line from the bottom)

Extract from Transcript. Direct Examination of Wilma by Prosecuting Attorney.

Q   Did he have on any kind of a hat ?   A   No.

Q   Was there anything particular about Johnnie's face
    that attracted your attention ?

A   I wasn't paying too much attention to him, but I think he had a scar or
    something; I don't know.

                                                p. 369.

Close examination of the photograph of Ernest Louis Charles Craine (Scar)
shows that he has a scar running from beneath his right nostril
diagonally to the edge of and center of his upper lip.

Although Wilma testified that she was not sure if
Johnnie had a facial scar, Father Wright took her
statement out of context. Wright also claimed to have
observed a scar underneath Craine's right nostril by
examining a mug shot under a student microscope.

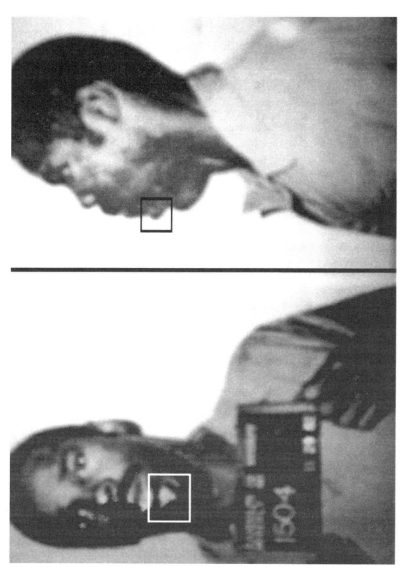

A June 1969 mug shot of Earnest "Scar" Craine shows that he had a large growth on his chin. Subsequent surgical procedures left a noticeable scar under his lower lip. Father Wright never saw this photo.

SPECULATION ABOUT WHAT HAPPENED ON 23 SEPTEMBER 1971
TO WILMA CHESTNUT ON KINGSBURY

Suggestion : Ernest Charles Craine (Louis, Spar) blinded Wilma.

Written: August 12 1972

Explanation: Wilma met Johnnie, Earl & Louis for the first time on the
day of the blinding. It's very likely that she confused
the two (Louis & Johnnie) in her mind. Ronnie, Earl &
Louis returned for the robbery — Wilma thought Louis was
Johnnie — maybe he used the name Johnnie to confuse her.
Louis choled Wilma with Earl's help; therefore he (Earl)
w$_a$s technically an accomplice. Louis then blinded Wilma,
either alone or in the presence of Earl & Ronnie. Then,
after bragging about it, he gave notice that he was running.
That left Earl & Ronnie to face the charges alone. Ronnie
wasn't about to get charged with the blinding, wanted
to avoid the robbery charges too, so he threatened Earl.
If Earl implicated him, he would say that Earl took part
in the blinding. Earl agreed to blame Johnnie —(Louis, too,
if caught, could implicate Earl in the blinding) Thus
Earl has a strong motive for lying about Johnnie.
    Laura visited Wilma in the hospital & explained that
Ronnie was totally innocent of the blinding. She got
Wilma to agree not to implicate him in the robbery. Wilma
believed that Louis (whom she knew as Johnnie) was her
attacker and saw no reason to involve Ronnie. So she
too had a motive (however well-intended) to lie about
Ronnie. Perhaps threats were somehow involved.

EVENTS SINCE AUGUST 12

1.   Photograph of Charles Craine obtained from police and taken 15 June 1971
show beginnings of flaring-out sideburns and scar in middle of
upper lip.

2.   Implications of Letters to Dasey of 9 november and 17 November 1971
dawned and between 2 & 5 Feb brought out in TRUTHTELLING ess$_a$y
written by Fr Ralph Wright around 2 Feb.

3.   8February. Wilma tells Mrs Drury that the THREE who came back were:
        RONNIE CLOWER   EARL HARPER   JOHNNIE BROOKS
and that Johnnie Brooks had long sideburns and a scar on his
lip. n She prefaced this by saying that she would only tell
this to Mrs Drury — not to any one else. When asked by Mrs Drury
whether the scar was on his face she said 'No, it was on his lip.'

4.   21 Feb   Wilma states in conversation to Mrs Drury that all
came back except Ronnie Clower — thus reverting to her original
statement made at the Trial. She still maintained that Johnnie
had a noticeable scar on his upper lip.

    NOTE On the 8 February she stated that one of the men who had
    been there earlier did not come back. She did not name
    . . .. o March 1973.

Father Wright deduced correctly that Wilma had confused
the facial features of Johnnie and Craine, but he assumed
that she did so as part of an elaborate plot to frame Johnnie.
He set out to "prove" that Wilma committed perjury.

Self-professed psychic healer Barbara Drury and *St. Louis Post-Dispatch* reporter George Curry devised a plan to record a conversation between Wilma and Drury to test Wright's theory that Wilma committed perjury. Wilma was not informed that she was being taped. Prosecutors later investigated the incident.

SLGD

Thanks to the generosity of St. Louisans and people all over the world, Wilma was able to move to a safe neighborhood after she recovered from her injuries. Thieves raided her former residence while she was hospitalized.

SLGD

Wilma takes a break after a long day at school.

Wilma waits to testify against Johnnie in yet another retrial. The first verdict was reversed on appeal; the second and third attempts ended in mistrials.

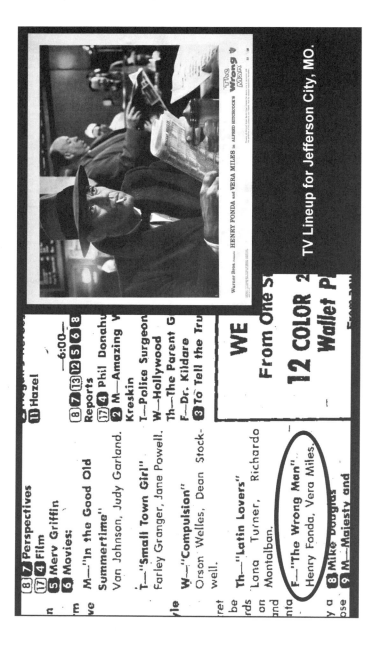

TV Lineup for Jefferson City, MO.

In an article sympathetic to Johnnie and written by *Post-Dispatch* reporter George Curry, Johnnie described himself as "the wrong man." The interview was conducted weeks after the Hitchcock classic by that title aired on TV in Jefferson City. Johnnie had never used the phrase before the movie aired.

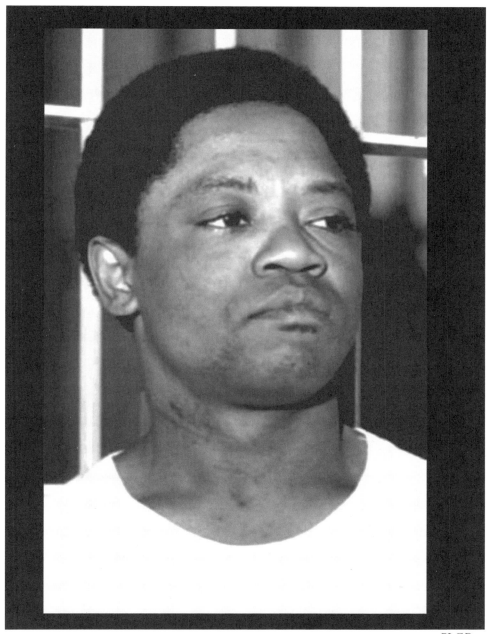

Johnnie Lee Brooks poses for newspaper photographers after recovering from a suicide attempt following his first conviction. Scars on the right side of his neck show the site of the minor injury caused by a razor hidden in his cell.

TO WILMA CHESTNUT AN OFFICIAL TRIBUTE

The martial arts are full of dedicated people who train hard, and those people know better than anybody that it takes such dedication to achieve success. In St. Louis there is a young woman named Wilma Chestnut who has redefined dedication and intensive training in terms that would shame many karatekas who only work out occasionally ... and even then not very hard.

About a year ago, Wilma had the misfortune to witness a crime and then suffer the horror of having the culprits blind her so that she could not identify them. A terrible atrocity in anyone's opinion, but Wilma decided that it was not going to keep her down. Her boyfriend was studying karate at the time at the Sen-no-Sen Dojo and, with the encouragement of her family and friends, she decided to talk to instructor Earl Rogers who convinced her to enroll.

At the present ti private lessons fr who decided to techniques, since ecuted after the o victim. It was slow at first, with Ro

technique on his student then showing her, by touch, how to do it herself. Wilma proved to be an excellent student and worked hard to master the movements. She says the hardest part was to learn to fall properly, no mean feat when you can't see the ground.

In addition to working out at the dojo every week, she is also a full-time student at nearby Forest Park Junior College. Down and out? Not by a long shot! Wilma comments that her family supports her in all her activities but that her mother did get quite upset recently when she and

Wilma, who took up karate after an attack that left her blind, was featured in a major martial arts magazine. Chuck Norris, a popular expert, was also featured.

SLGD

Wilma walks to class at St. Louis University as fellow students look on.

Craine's testimony finally demonstrated why Wilma confused the facial features of two men who robbed her. Earl covered her eyes as Johnnie choked her.

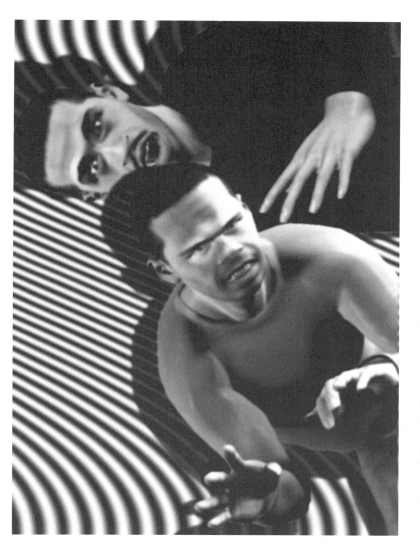

After exiting the bathroom, Craine saw Johnnie choking Wilma. She passed out as he grabbed Johnnie's left arm. He thought she was dead.

CHAPTER 13

Appeal

Wright had gotten wind that the verdict was going to be overturned days before it was publicly disclosed. In preparation for the new trial, he created the "Johnnie Brooks Legal Defense Fund" and began contacting prominent defense attorneys to take over Johnnie's case.

Thanks to him, Johnnie's luck in beating the legal system continued.

Despite being unable to afford a lawyer, he snared Norman S. London, a man regarded as one of the best criminal attorneys in the country. Prosecutors dreaded facing him.

London graduated from the Washington University School of Law in St. Louis in 1950. Eager to join the ranks of F. Lee Bailey and Edward Bennett Williams as a feared and fearless defense attorney, he took cases that other lawyers considered lost causes.

What they missed and what London saw was the immense media attention drawn in such cases.

In October 1959, for example, the St. Louis Zoo paid Miami animal trainer Robert Tomarchin $1,600 to bring his "talking" chimpanzee to the zoo as a summer tourism magnet.

They made the offer after seeing Tomarchin on the "Ed Sullivan Show" and "Wild Kingdom," where "Moke the Talking Monkey" amazed the nation with his ability to say "momma" and a few other words.

Once the weather turned cold and the visitors were gone, Tomarchin accused the zoo of neglecting Moke's living conditions.

In a fit of rage, Tomarchin broke into the zoo one night before Christmas, kidnapped the monkey, and left a cashier's check for $1,000. He promised to send the $600 balance soon.

Since the trainer was clearly guilty, most defense lawyers didn't want to hurt their reputations by championing a hopeless cause. London accepted it. He arranged for the trainer to return the ape.

During the trial, London argued that his client had literally "fallen in love" with Moke and as such, he deserved leniency for his crime of passion.

Fortunately, the public was sympathetic and didn't want to see the trainer go to jail. All they wanted was to see Moke back at the zoo. By contrast, the zoo's attorneys demanded prison time as a warning to other potential thieves.

"Moke is the only thing I ever loved," Tomarchin told the judge moments before receiving a four-year sentence instead of the 15-year maximum.

Even though it was not technically a win since Tomarchin did not get off scot-free, his sentence was much lighter than another attorney might have obtained.

The victory for London was the publicity. The case generated national and international headlines and put London's name on the map. Reporters began monitoring his caseload, hoping to find another potentially sensational trial.

London made headlines again in October after his clients, whose only defense was a weak alibi, were acquitted of robbery. William Bailey Ferguson and his wife, who lived in Little Rock, were positive that London's clients were the two men who broke into their home days before Christmas 1957, tied them up, and then robbed them of $12,000. Several friends of the defendants testified that they saw both men in Potomac, Missouri on the day the crime was committed.

London caused another sensation when he began representing organized crime figures in the St. Louis area.

In May 1968, he angered the local black community after helping police organize to protest the suspension of four officers in the brutal beating of Charles Koen and Leon Dent, leaders of a black activist group called the Black Liberators.

The men were inside a police station following their arrests on a minor traffic violation, so there were no eyewitnesses.

In May 1971, he represented a student war protester accused of attempting to burn down the ROTC building on the Washington University campus.

London hired Chester J. "Chet" Pleban, a recent graduate of the St. Louis University School of Law, to assist him with Johnnie's defense. In May, the retrial was put on the docket for June 17.

Since Johnnie made a big stink about his original trial lawyers being inexperienced and for refusing to let him take the stand, the state wasn't leaving anything to chance.

He had the best lawyer possible, and he was getting another opportunity to take the stand to give his version of events. If convicted again, he wouldn't have those red herrings on appeal.

The judge granted a continuance on June 17 to give London time to take depositions and otherwise prepare for trial.

It also turned out to be a blessing for the prosecution, whose entire case centered around Wilma's faulty identification testimony and Earl's conflict of interest problem.

The long hunt for Earnest "Scar" Craine ended ten days later. The FBI had tracked him down.

The St. Louis police department received word on June 27 that Scar had been apprehended in San Francisco. He was convicted on a drug charge in 1972 after Johnnie's trial was over, and was convicted of burglary in 1973.

The warrant for Scar's arrest was forgotten after Johnnie's first trial. Prosecutors renewed their effort to locate him as an act of desperation. They were afraid of relying solely upon Earl or Wilma to make their case. No new physical evidence had been discovered.

They wanted victory insurance, and Scar was it.

Sergeant Francis Sullivan of the fugitive section flew to San Francisco on June 28 and brought him to St. Louis on July 1. Two detectives questioned him on videotape the same afternoon. After confessing his role in the robbery, he was formally arrested and sent to lockup.

The new trial set for August 12 but was postponed again at London's request. He wanted more depositions in the wake of Scar's arrest.

Earl had gotten into trouble in the meantime, and was in the penitentiary serving 30 months for burglary. He was transferred to the City Jail a few days before the second trial started on September 30.

When the court was called to session, the judge shocked everyone by declaring a mistrial.

The culprit was an article in the *St. Louis Post-Dispatch* that morning. The new trial judge felt it was prejudicial to both sides. The prosecutor was under the impression that neither the *Post-Dispatch* nor the *Globe-Democrat* would publish anything about the retrial until the jury was sworn.

Reporters told the judge, however, that they were not aware of any such agreement.

The next trial was set for November 12. London and Pleban sat at the defense table across from Fredericks and Marion Eisen, an assistant prosecutor who had been an exemplary student at the St. Louis University School of Law. In fact, she and Pleban both graduated in the class of 1974.

Fredericks said in his opening statement that Wilma would positively identify Brooks as the man who assaulted and later blinded her. He also promised that Earl and Scar would corroborate her testimony and would reveal in detail what happened after Wilma passed out from choking.

In his opening, London charged that it would be impossible for Wilma to positively identify Johnnie as the man who blinded her for the very reason that the prosecutor had stated: she was unconscious at the time and couldn't possibly know who did it.

London made several specious arguments before the trial got under way. He wanted the court to bar Ronnie Clower from testifying about Johnnie's request for a knife because no knife was used to cut Wilma.

He knew full well that it established Johnnie's premeditation or intent to commit armed robbery, but it also bore directly on the question of whether Johnnie was the one who cut Wilma.

Since no one saw Johnnie slash Wilma's eyes with the broken glass, London also wanted testimony barred about someone blinding her in the course of robbing her. He implied that she could have fallen down and somehow blinded herself in the process.

"It is our position that there is no independent evidence of an assault and the cutting of her eyes," he said.

"It isn't necessary that we have a witness to the assault," Fredericks replied. "We can establish that an assault was, in fact, committed."

The indictment charged Johnnie with using "an unknown sharp instrument," and a knife certainly fits that description. The prosecutors planned to prove by the testimony of Dr. Reginald McKinney and others that Wilma's eyes were deliberately cut.

London countered that Dr. McKinney was unable to prove that her eyes were cut as part of the crime.

When Lillie took the stand, she said that police did not come to her apartment to interview her until seven o'clock that evening. They did not gather any evidence.

In questioning Lillie Harry, London discovered a major mistake in Father's Wright's contention that an independent source overheard Wilma tell Harry that "Ronnie did it." He was hoping to prove that both Lillie and a man named John Phillips overheard Wilma say that.

However, the monk had given London bad information. Phillips was not simply someone who happened to be nearby. He was not even there when Harry arrived or by the time she left. He had come later.

Phillips was dating Colia, and they had been together for some time. He went to the hospital that day because Colia called him. She was frantic and he became concerned that she was having an emotional breakdown.

The only thing he told police was that Wilma had mentioned someone named Ronnie being in the apartment at some point.

All London ended up proving was that the police reports were inaccurate, that Wright had misinterpreted them, and that the only person who claimed to have evidence of Wilma stating "Ronnie did it" was the self-styled evangelist Barbara Drury.

Bettye Simmons, the woman who lived across the hall from Lillie, was among the first to testify. She said that she "could see dried blood" on Wilma's eyes, which essentially established why there was no blood on Johnnie's clothing.

Wilma was lying flat on her back at the time her eyes were cut, and bleeding was minimal. It would not likely have been on her assailant's clothing.

His hands had blood on them only because he cut through the eyelid of the right eye, but lifted the eyelid on the left eye before cutting it.

Bleeding from the cuts was very limited. It had coagulated within 30 minutes of the assault.

London's strategy was to try to discredit key witnesses by showing that they made one statement to the grand jury or police three years earlier and were giving different statements now.

For example, Lillie told the grand jury that it was about 3:10 when she returned home from job hunting. Now she was testifying that it was about 3:15 or 3:30.

His point, he said, was that she didn't know what time she left that morning or what time she returned. But instead of discrediting her, it sounded as though he was badgering the witness.

London was experienced enough to know that people forget minor details over time. Nearly every witness had forgotten details.

Officer Jerome Dampier, for instance, described the sofa in the living room as a sleep sofa. "I guess it was a couch that lets out into a bed." He was wrong. He assumed that because the pillows to the sofa were on the floor.

Johnnie had removed them from the sofa and laid Wilma on top of them in an attempt to rape her. But if Dampier had inspected it more closely, he would have noticed that the sofa was a just a wooden frame with six pillows on it, three for sitting on and three for back support.

He also testified that there were three children in the apartment when there were only two. Those mistakes did not nullify the truthful core of his testimony and jurors knew that.

Johnnie told Father Wright that picking up Ronnie Clower on the morning of the attack was a fluke. Ronnie's testimony suggested other-wise. Johnnie planned to pick up Ronnie and take him to enlist in the Marines. When he arrived, Sammie was in the car.

Johnnie introduced Sammie to Ronnie as his cousin.

Ronnie testified further than when they returned from the Chrysler plant in Fenton, it was around 8:30. Johnnie stopped at a tavern and bought a quart of beer after he dropped off Sammie. They drank the beer and started discussing women.

Both were married, but they had roving eyes. After Ronnie mentioned that his girlfriend had a friend named Wilma, Johnnie expressed a desire to meet her.

They drove to Wilma's house and found out that she was elsewhere. Johnnie picked up Earl and Scar. By the time they arrived at Kingsbury, it was about 11:45, he said.

Johnnie stopped to buy cigarettes or gas on the way home. It was around 12:45, he testified.

Ronnie arrived at his mother's house, at which point Johnnie requested a knife. He removed a knife from a kitchen drawer and headed back downstairs to give it to Johnnie.

His mother became hysterical because she had a bad feeling about Johnnie. She started yelling and screaming at him about running the streets. By the time Ronnie reached the front door, his mother was crying loudly and begging him not to go with Johnnie.

Ronnie told the trio that he couldn't go. They pleaded with him to go because he was their only sure means of getting Wilma to let them in. When they pulled off, Ronnie went to his wife's house to see his children.

He spent a few hours there, and then went to his brother's house on Green Lea, and then went home. That's why Johnnie couldn't find him on the evening of the attack.

Since London failed to block Ronnie's testimony about the knife, he tried to discredit him by arguing that his testimony conflicted with the statement he gave police on September 23.

Ronnie denied giving detectives the statement in their report. Despite being in custody for two hours, Ronnie said that their questions were mainly about with whom he spent time that day.

They held him until Johnnie arrived at the police station. He refuted London's contention that he was interviewed and gave a detailed statement.

"They just asked me did I know Johnnie Brooks," he replied. "If that is an interview, I guess so."

His reply apparently baffled London. The more London tried to discredit Ronnie, the more questions he raised about the accuracy of the police report.

London asked Ronnie if it was true that he said "that you were driving in a car and you first saw Wilma Chestnut on the corner of Laurel and Westminster?"

"No," Ronnie replied.

"You did not make that statement?" London shot back.

"No," he answered.

The unequivocal denial caught London off guard. He had failed to subpoena the officers who took Ronnie's alleged statement.

A first-rate lawyer would have had the police there ready to contradict him. The defense was starting to fall apart because London had banked on the accuracy of the police reports.

Hoping to portray Ronnie as a nefarious type, London asked about his criminal background. Ronnie told him that he had never been arrested for anything, so the tactic backfired.

London's last hope for salvaging something from Ronnie's testimony was to have him describe the three people he had taken to see Wilma. Earl wore a purple shirt and purple pants, he said. Louis (Scar) wore a Levi's jean jacket and Levi's blue jeans. Johnnie wore overalls.

The defense plan called for Ronnie and Wilma being discredited by their alleged statements to police on September 23 and 24.

Detectives had filed a report stating that they interviewed Wilma at Homer G. Phillips on the afternoon of September 24.

The doctor who told them that Wilma was lucid enough to be interviewed had overestimated her stability.

Wilma was still despondent the day after she was blinded. She would be aware of her surroundings one minute and would return to a semi-conscious state the next.

Apparently the detectives constructed the statements allegedly made by Wilma and Ronnie from interviews with Colia, Lillie, and a few others. They surveyed the neighborhood to get an idea of where the school stood in relation to the apartment. The strange thing about both statements is that they read almost identically.

A key red flag in the statements is the contention that Wilma encountered Ronnie while she was walking Herbert to school. The only problem was that Wilma never walked Herbert to school. The children in the neighborhood walked in groups to school and were rarely chaperoned by an adult.

The school was only a block away from Lillie's apartment.

The reports noted that Herbert came home for lunch without being escorted by Wilma, and returned to school without her escorting him. So why would she have escorted him to school in the morning when she was watching the babies?

She didn't. The police did not get that statement from Wilma.

London wanted to ask Ronnie questions about the day he was interviewed by police, but the judge told him blocked it. He would only allow the questioning if London could prove that he had at least one witness ready to testify that Wilma said "Ronnie did it."

Fredericks objected to the line of questioning because he knew that no such witness existed. London was not telling the truth.

COURT: Is somebody coming into the courtroom [to] say she said that?"

LONDON: I don't remember who the witness was, but several witnesses –

FREDERICKS: If he can't pin it down as to who said it, it would be hearsay.

LONDON: Wilma said it . . . made the statement "Ronnie did it."

COURT: Wilma said it? Is she going to say that she said it?

FREDERICKS: No, sir, nor can he find that in any transcript or police report.

London had fallen into a trap set by Father Wright and Barbara Drury to snare Wilma, and he had no one to blame but himself.

Drury was the only person to claim that Wilma made such a statement. Wright took her word as gospel and relayed the allegation to the defense team.

Now London's reputation was on the line. He had nothing to prove the bogus allegation that Wilma committed perjury.

Drury had also given Father Wright the impression that she was present at the hospital when Wilma made the statement about Ronnie. No police report mentions her presence.

Besides that, no one but immediate family members were allowed to see Wilma, so there was no way Drury could have visited her. Any white visitor would have been conspicuous in the all-black hospital.

CHAPTER 14

Half Truths

Wilma was called next.

Colia escorted her to the stand and then took a seat behind the prosecutor's table. She told the court that Johnnie was flirtatious from the moment he entered the apartment. He talked about his alleged job as a mechanic at a gas station, and he bragged about hanging around near Vandeventer and St. Ferdinand, which everyone knew was gang territory.

She reiterated her testimony about Johnnie begging for water because he had a hot box. She was very convincing until she described the actions of the three men accused of robbing her.

WILMA: "We talked and every now and then I would ask "Where's Ronnie?" and they would say "He is down the street talking to the girl." Then Earl and Louis started getting up [and] going outside, coming back

115

in and after a while I just told them to leave; it was time for them to go because I was getting ready to dress."

She described Louis as a dark-skinned male about 6'1" with short hair. He was dressed in dark clothing and a black leather coat. He seemed to be about 21 years old. She didn't observe any facial hair.

The defense knew that Scar always sported a moustache.

Earl was a slim teenager who wore an Afro. She wondered why he was hanging around with guys so much older than himself. He wore purple pants and a purple jersey.

Johnnie wore a green jersey and Levi's jeans, she said. His open shirt made him look like he had broad shoulders and a skinny waist and hips. He sported lamb chop sideburns and he might have had a scar on his face, but she wasn't sure. He stood about 5'10" tall. Johnnie said that he was 27 but he looked closer to 30.

Reporters noted that Johnnie smiled when Wilma made that statement. She clearly had mistaken him for Earnest "Scar" Craine.

Dr. Reginald McKinney was called to the stand. London gambled with the jury's respect when he questioned him. He twisted the physician's words to suggest that Wilma might have fallen and somehow blinded herself in the process. He noted that McKinney had already testified that Wilma had injured the back of her head and that blood was found there.

LONDON: And you testified, have you not, that a fall could have caused these [eye] injuries that Miss Chestnut suffered. Is that not your testimony?

FREDERICKS: Your Honor, it was not his testimony. This was a question.

In fact, McKinney was responding to a wild hypothetical question when he mentioned that a fall might have caused the injuries. His reply, basically, was that *anything is possible*, but it certainly was not probable. London had knowingly taken his reply out of context and Fredericks nailed him on it.

Besides, the line of questioning was an insult to the jury's intelligence. A smart lawyer would never have tried to impeach McKinney's testimony about the cuts unless he had another physician ready to testify that the wounds were consistent with a fall.

The moment that everyone was waiting for came when Earnest Charles Craine took the stand. It was impossible to find the whole truth without hearing from everyone involved. Craine was the missing puzzle piece.

He said that he was alone with Wilma for about 15 to 20 minutes after Earl and Johnnie went to buy a quart of beer. He grew tired of waiting and decided to leave, telling Wilma to advise them of that when they returned. He never touched her during that time.

He ran into them as soon as he left the building, however, and the three went back upstairs. Craine left in the first place because he had to use the bathroom. He asked Wilma's permission and she said yes.

When he came out, he saw Johnnie choking Wilma and saw Earl placing his hands over her eyes. He grabbed Johnnie by the shoulder and they scuffled.

"I pulled Brooks off her," he said. "I thought she was dead."

"I know what I'm doing," Johnnie said angrily. "She's only knocked out."

Devannie, the baby that Wilma had sat on the sofa between herself and Johnnie was "crying, hollering and screaming" as Wilma struggled for her life, he said.

Johnnie ordered him and Earl to grab the record player and tape recorder and leave. The color TV was too large and heavy, so they decided not to steal it. Johnnie said that he would meet them outside after he "took care" of Wilma.

He came downstairs about ten minutes later.

They saw blood on his hands. When they asked whether he had killed her, Johnnie replied that he had not. He said that he "cut her eyes out" to prevent her from identifying them.

Johnnie tossed the car keys to Earl and instructed him to drive to a nearby house. Someone inside the white bungalow gave Johnnie $25 or $30 for the merchandise.

Johnnie offered him five dollars, Scar said, but he refused to take it. He offered Earl the same amount, but Scar wasn't sure if Earl accepted it. He didn't see Johnnie again for three days.

During that time, he and Earl discussed what Johnnie had done. Johnnie had committed crimes that neither of them anticipated, and now they had to figure out how to distance themselves from him.

"He said that Johnnie was crazy to do what he did," Scar told the silent courtroom, "when he didn't have to do it."

Afraid that all three of them would be charged for hurting Wilma, Scar said that he fled to Los Angeles.

London was unable to find anything in Craine's testimony to attack. He exposed Craine's criminal history, but it only proved that Scar had never committed a crime against another person. All of his offenses involved breaking into vending machines or public intoxication.

London also tried unsuccessfully to block *Post-Dispatch* reporter Ronald J. Lawrence from testifying. The reporter had conducted a half-hour interview on October 7. At the time, Johnnie was chained to a bed in a special section at City Hospital Number One on Lafayette.

Johnnie told Lawrence that he couldn't have been involved because he was at the Chrysler plant in Fenton at the time. His car suffered a blow-out.

If the reporter wanted to confirm this, Johnnie told him where to look for the bad tire that he tossed on the shoulder of the road. When the reporter expressed skepticism, Johnnie said that he couldn't have done it because he was in jail on a robbery charge on September 23 and was not released until after the crime was committed.

Lawrence did something that reporter George Curry, psychic Barbara Drury and Father Wright failed to do: he checked police records and discovered that Johnnie was lying.

With his lies exposed, Johnnie no longer had an alibi.

Prosecutors called Earl Harper as their final witness. Scar and Earl were both represented by the same public defender, Joseph Warzycki.

Fredericks was assured at the beginning of the trial that Earl would testify. But after conferring with his attorney, Earl changed his mind and pleaded the Fifth Amendment. Since he had no deal this time, he might face as much as 15 years imprisonment on a revised charge.

The supervisor at the reformatory where Earl was serving time said later that "he would have signed his own death warrant if he testified." Don Hartness, acting supervisor at the reformatory, said that inmates dealt harshly with any inmate who cooperated with prosecutors.

Without Earl's testimony, Judge J. Casey Walsh had no alternative but to declare a mistrial.

Prosecutors said that they would seek a new trial immediately, but that was the last thing the Chestnut family wanted to hear.

It appeared that Johnnie was right when he said that blinding Wilma would prevent any of her attackers from going to jail.

In preparation for the new trial, Johnnie's legal team had relied upon the word of a self-proclaimed faith healer who seemed allergic to the truth and a monk on a quixotic crusade. When prosecutors discovered this, they decided to give Johnnie's defenders a taste of their own medicine.

After the second mistrial, Fredericks had subpoenas served on evangelist Barbara Drury, Father Ralph Wright, and George Curry of the *Post-Dispatch*. Drury and Wright were scheduled to appear on December 13 in the Circuit Court Attorney's office.

Although both Fredericks and London were present during the deposition, London stated before the questioning began that he had a standing objection "to each and every question asked and each and every answer given."

Since a notice of appeal was pending, he said, the court lacked jurisdiction or authority to order anyone deposed pending the outcome of the appeal. His objection was overruled.

After taking the oath, Drury testified that she was an ordained minister in something called the "Evangelistic Association."

Asked if she had any formal education qualifying her as a minister, Drury initially responded with gobbledygook.

"I had the gift of healing," she replied, and "after healing many people over the phone and through letters, I became ordained."

Realizing that Drury did not understand what he meant by "formal education," Fredericks asked her whether any of her formal education included matriculation at an accredited college or university.

"No," she replied.

When asked how she became involved in the case, Drury stated that Jim Brown, a Belridge County police officer doing investigative work for Father Wright approached her. Wright, she added, had also brought Johnnie's mother to seek her counsel.

Brown, Drury said, had uncovered information indicating that Johnnie was framed.

Oddly, Drury was the first person to note under oath that Earl Harper lived next door to Johnnie's mother. Logistically, prosecutors should have been pointed that out to the jury during the first trial. It was a major oversight, and so was the failure to reinforce this geographical nexus by diagrams or illustrations.

By the same token, prosecutors failed to drive home the point that Scar lived directly across the street from Earl and Johnnie.

Once he established Drury's lack of credentials in criminal procedure, Fredericks honed in on the reason for deposing her.

"Did you ever talk to Wilma Chestnut?"

"I know her personally," Drury replied.

"That's not the question," Fredericks retorted.

Asked whether she had ever talked to Wilma on the phone and recorded the conversation, Drury replied that she had.

"Do you have that recording?"

"No," she replied. "I destroyed it."

"Did you play it to anyone before you destroyed it?"

"Well," she said, "what's his name from the *Post*."

After Fredericks volunteered several names, Drury identified George Curry as the person who heard the tape.

Curry was working on a story about Johnnie, she said, and he broached the idea of calling Wilma and recording the conversation.

While she placed the taping idea on Curry, she failed to note that the idea came up only after Drury claimed to have "proof" that Wilma gave perjured testimony against Johnnie.

Days before his interview with Johnnie, she said, Curry said he wanted to bring an eavesdropping device to her home in order to record a conversation between herself and Wilma.

Realizing the importance of what Drury was admitting, Fredericks got excited, so much so that Drury noticed it.

"How did he put it on your phone?" he asked.

"Well," she said, "there is you know . . . are you getting nervous?"

"No, ma'am," he replied. "I always do this. How did he put it on your phone?"

"Well, you know," she said, "those little suction pieces that you put on the receiver."

After the tape recorder was set up with the eavesdropping device, Drury said she called Wilma. She never told Wilma that she was recording the conversation.

As Wilma was about to end the call, Drury requested permission to tape their conversation. Wilma said absolutely not.

"And was George Curry there during [the taping]?"

"Yes," Drury answered.

"Did he hear the words that you were speaking into the phone or was he in close proximity to hear them, to hear what you were saying?"

"Yes."

With those answers, London knew that Fredericks had a powerful weapon for use in the new trial. The taping clearly violated wiretapping laws, exposing everyone who heard it to possible prosecution.

London said nothing. Drury's next series of answers may explain why.

She said that she destroyed the tape because she did not "feel I should have the tape."

"Did you play it for anyone else before you destroyed it?" he asked.

"I think Mr. London's lawyer heard it," she said.

Fredericks explained to her that London was a lawyer and did not have a lawyer, so she could not have played it for such a person. He assumed that she was referring to one of the lawyers working with him on Johnnie's defense.

At the time, Chet Pleban was co-counsel, so perhaps she was referring to him. Fredericks did not ask that question, however, and Pleban said recently that he does not recollect hearing the tape.

Drury's replies suggested that she destroyed the tape immediately after recording it, but she admitted that she kept the recording for more than a month before allegedly burning it.

She testified that no one else heard the tape except "London's lawyer."

"Is he the only one you played the tape for?" Fredericks asked for clarity.

"Yes," she answered.

"*No one else*, is that correct?"

"Yes."

When asked about her alleged friendship with Wilma, Drury testified that they became friends after she sponsored a "gospel concert that raised over "$2,000 for her."

In fact, records show that Drury's concert raised about five hundred dollars. Wilma and her family received the funds in an Old Judge coffee can.

Drury also said that her son Jim (who had dated Wilma's roommate Carolyn Renn) had questioned Wilma about the names of the people who came to Kingsbury during the second visit on the day she was blinded.

He raised the questions informally at a breakfast that Mayor Cervantes held to honor Drury for her work in prisons. She was known as the "Jailhouse Angel."

Drury also exaggerated the nature of her relationship with Wilma's mother, Colia.

"Did you ever talk with Mrs Chestnut, Wilma's mother?"

"Yes," she replied. "I know her very well."

"Do you remember what the conversation was between you and Colia Chestnut?" Fredericks inquired.

"Who?" Drury answered, clearly puzzled by the name.

"Her name is C-O-L-I —"

"C-O-R-A," Drury replied.

"Cora?" Fredericks asked.

"I believe," she said.

Clearly, she did not know Colia well, any more than she knew Wilma well. Anyone familiar with Colia knew that her name was pronounced "Col-ya" or "CO-lee-uh." No one ever called her Cora, close friends called her "Cola-Ru."

It had only taken an hour or so for Fredericks to realize something that Johnnie's lawyers failed to: you had to take any information from Drury with a grain of salt.

In his opening argument during the second trial, London promised the jury that he would prove that Wilma made the statement "Ronnie did it" to at least one witness for the defense.

When Fredericks called his bluff, London backed down. The only witness who ever claimed to have heard Wilma say that was Drury. As he wrapped up his deposition of her, he demonstrated how Drury had once again stretched the truth to suit her own ends.

"Do you recall what the conversations were between Wilma's mother and yourself pertaining to this incident?" he asked.

"Yes," Barbara replied. "She told me that Wilma repeated three times that Ronnie did it when they brought her into the emergency room."

Father Wright had been operating under the impression that Drury was at the hospital visiting Wilma on the day after the assault and heard her say "Ronnie did it" three times.

Now the truth was out. Drury had not been anywhere near Homer G. Phillips on the day after the blinding. No one ever heard Wilma say "Ronnie did it."

What they heard, and what the trial testimony showed, is that Wilma only uttered two words when she was in the emergency room. Nearly every question was answered in a rhythmic "Ronnie, Ronnie, Ronnie" or "nobody, nobody, nobody."

London realized too late that he had been bamboozled. Asked if he had any questions for Drury, London replied: "No questions."

Father Wright was called to the stand after Fredericks was done with Drury. He testified that he had interviewed both Earl and Johnnie before the first trial.

The monk said that he tried to remember as much as possible about his two conversations with Earl. Since he did not take notes or record the conversation at the city jail, he reduced them to notes later.

Wright claimed that Earl made several statements suggesting that Johnny was being framed. Asked to read from his notes about those conversations, Wright said in part:

"They will never catch Scar. He won't be back until this case is over. I will take time for the tape deck but not for anything else. . . I am going to get out of this any way I can. And there are four people involved in this thing whose names I haven't even told my lawyer because I don't want to get them involved."

Wright deduced from those conversations that four more people were involved in addition to the four already suspected. He was never able to determine who Earl meant when he said "Wilma's cousin" knew.

Nor did he or the investigators working for Johnnie determine whether Earl merely meant that he had not given police the names of Ronnie and Scar.

Logically, that is what he meant by the four people. In his court testimony, for example, he does not mention Scar. Nor does he suggest that Ronnie was involved in any way.

(Even today, Wilma has no clue about any "cousin" being involved.)

The oddest thing about Wright's transcripts is that he seems to agree with Richard Wuestling's assessment of Earl as a "congenital liar," yet he believes that everything Earl told him was true where it exonerated Johnnie.

The other oddity is that he chose not to transcribe the third and last conversation with Earl wherein the youth suggested that Johnnie was guilty and deserved to be convicted for blinding Wilma.

It is as though he did not want to transcribe anything that refutes his conviction that Johnnie was framed by four key conspirators – Wilma, Ronnie, Earl, and Scar.

His notes suggests that one of them was Laura, Wilma's best friend and Ronnie's girlfriend. He speculated in his notes that Laura went to the hospital on the day of the blinding and convinced Wilma to stop saying that Ronnie was involved. This, like much else in his notes, was fantasy.

CHAPTER 15

Strike Three

Wright testified that Drury told him that Wilma told her (he was clearly unfamiliar with hearsay rules) that the three people who returned during the second visit were Ronnie, Earl and Johnnie. Her description of Johnnie, he noted, was actually consistent with Scar's features.

That's what he found troubling about Wilma's testimony, and that's why he believed that Johnnie was innocent.

Wilma told Drury, he said, and later testified that "Johnnie Brooks had the scar on his upper lip and that he had sideburns. And it was clear to me from this that Johnnie Brooks in her mind was not the Johnnie Brooks that I know from the description."

Following up on Drury's testimony about the taped telephone conversation, Fredericks asked Wright whether he was aware of any such conversations.

He replied that he was aware of "a phone call between Barbara Drury and Wilma Chestnut."

"How did you gain knowledge of that phone call?" Fredericks asked.

"Because she told me afterwards," he replied, "and in fact I heard part of the recording over the phone. She called me and played it to me over the phone. I couldn't hear it in great detail, but I did actually hear that recording."

Somebody was lying, and under oath.

"Do you know where that recording is now," Fredericks asked, "to the best of your information?"

"I suspect Barbara Drury has it," he answered.

According to Wright, Drury was the only person in whom Wilma confided that Johnnie Brooks had never come back to Kingsbury after the first visit.

He knew this because Drury told him and Curry. That's why the phone tap was suggested in the first place, to catch Wilma allegedly confiding in Drury again.

Drury also told him, he said, that she was at the hospital on the day after the attack and personally heard Wilma say "Ronnie did it" three times.

However, Drury told a different story under oath that day. She made no mention of visiting Wilma.

After giving Fredericks the wrong first name for Wilma's mother, Drury testified that Colia told her that "Wilma repeated three times that 'Ronnie did it' when they brought her into the emergency room."

The statement was misleading at best.

The depositions revealed that the monk had accepted Drury's words as gospel, just as he had taken Johnnie's 3,000-word confession as gospel. In turn, Johnnie's defense team accepted Father Wright's claims as the gospel truth for no other reason than his being a man of the cloth.

(Curry was scheduled to appear on January 8, 1975. His deposition was either missing or misplaced from the case file in the court archives at last check. However, Curry said during interviews that he recalled hearing the tape shortly before visiting Johnnie at the Missouri Penitentiary.)

Scar was indicted on one count of felony robbery after he was apprehended. His trial began on January 22.

Unable to get a deal due to the prosecution's fiasco with Earl, Scar pleaded guilty after the prosecution presented its case against him. He received a sentence of 12 years in the Missouri Penitentiary on February 21 and started serving time the next day.

Since Wilma knew nothing about the law, she never publicly criticized the prosecution's handling of the case. The trials and mistrials had taken their toll. Privately, she held concerns about yet another one.

She wondered how Johnnie had been able to win so much sympathy from the media and the courts less than two years after one of the most heinous crimes in the state's history.

She wondered about some of the prosecution's strategies but assumed that they knew how to make the best presentation. She was surprised, for example, that Fredericks sent her home the first two days of the first trial. After she testified on the third day, he requested that she stay away from the court until the jury began deliberating.

Why didn't he have her available outside the courtroom merely for the sake of reminding the public of what those charged had done to her? Why hadn't he done role-playing and role reversal to prepare her?

While Fredericks asked her some questions about her testimony, he did not have mock court sessions the way top-notch lawyers do. If an attorney or prosecutor fails to brief a client, they end up asking questions that precipitate unpleasant answers. This usually results in a defeat.

Thus the adage of lawyers: never ask a question for which you don't already know the answer.

Wilma had remembered certain characteristics of the three men simply by how the brain categorizes and compartmentalizes information. Earl, for instance, was the youngest and the smallest, she noted. He was so cockeyed, she recalled, that it was a wonder he could walk straight.

Johnnie was taller and heavier than Earl, and Scar was slightly taller and heavier than Johnnie. Scar had a face that was difficult to forget because, as his nickname suggests, he had a noticeable scar.

A 1969 mug shot shows that Scar had a large fluid-filled growth under his lower lip. A large crease ran along the left side of the growth. He had surgery the following year to remove it, but it left a noticeable keloidal scar.

She also wondered why Johnnie hung around with a kid if he was such a big man. Johnnie kept saying his name and trying to court her while telling his life story. She remembered his unquenchable thirst and that he educated them all about the meaning of a "hot box."

She didn't know that Johnnie had not bathed in three days but his body odor suggested that he had poor hygiene. He smelled awful (the result of not bathing and working on cars in summer heat).

Johnnie started choking her as Earl stood by the front door. Scar was in the bathroom.

The first time Johnnie choked her, Wilma was able to pull his hand away by grabbing him by the wrists. He had underestimated her strength. She was holding his hands away from her neck when Earl grabbed her from behind and pulled her backward.

As he pulled her backward, she fell across the hard wooden edge of the sofa and hurt her back. She lost her grip on Johnnie's wrists as she tried to figure out how to fight both of them. She got dizzy as Johnnie tightened his grip around her neck.

She could see her entire life flash before her eyes. Just as she thought she was about to die, she looked up once more to try to figure out why the man she had been so kind to moments ago was trying to kill her.

As she was losing consciousness, she heard someone yell something long forgotten.

She looked up one final time. She saw two faces in the dizzy haze before passing out. The last face she remembered seeing had a scar on it, but it was not the face of her attacker. Her attacker's *shirt was open*.

The fourth trial for Johnnie Lee Brooks got underway on April 24 before Judge Harold R. Satz.

Scar refused to testify for fear of receiving more time under the new theory of the case, but also because he felt that prosecutors should have recommended a shorter sentence following his guilty plea.

With Warzycki still acting as his attorney, Scar took the Fifth Amendment.

Since he refused to testify, prosecutors used his testimony from the last trial. London had cross-examined Scar during the last trial. For that reason, his objection to the prosecution submitting the earlier testimony was overruled.

Fredericks presented a much clearer chronology of events in his opening statement.

He emphasized that Wilma's blindness could not have been the result of an accident, as London suggested, because the cuts across her pupils were straight across each one. There was no cut or laceration on the bridge of her nose, nor was there any evidence that she sustained injury to any other part of her face.

The cuts, he said, were a deliberate attempt by Johnnie to prevent her from identifying the people who robbed her. As such, the assault was a part of the robbery and not a separate crime.

Lillie Harry was a very nervous when she took the stand. When London started raising questions about discrepancies between her testimony now and years ago, she grew even more anxious.

When he started asking questions about Herbert's interview with the police, she nearly lost her composure. She didn't want him to testify because he was deathly afraid of Johnnie.

He told her that he feared Johnnie would cut his eyes out if he testified against him. Fortunately, London dropped the line of questioning about Herbert and moved on.

The defense presented only four witnesses before resting its case on Friday, the second day of the trial.

Brendan Ryan, head of the city attorney's office, announced on the last day of the trial – a rare Saturday session – that prosecutors were dropping the assault charge against Johnnie in order to avoid the possibility of yet another mistrial.

Instead, Ryan said, the prosecution would proceed "with the robbery charge on the theory that we will show that the assault occurred as part of the robbery."

Since a reporter had blown Johnnie's alibi to shreds at the last trial, the defense devised a new theory of the case.

In his opening statement, London argued that the evidence would show that Scar was the person who blinded Wilma. Johnnie, he said, never returned to apartment after the first visit. Evidence would also show that Ronnie was the one who returned to the apartment with Scar and Earl.

He argued that the reason Scar used a fake name of "Louis" was that he had already decided to rob Wilma before going to the apartment that afternoon.

He blinded her to prevent her from identifying him. Wilma's testimony would prove, he said, that Scar fit the description of the person she thought was Johnnie.

Scar fled to Los Angeles to avoid prosecution, he said. He used the alias of Ernest Speaks to obtain new identification papers that helped him evade capture for two years. He kept in contact with his sister in St. Louis to monitor the case against Johnnie.

This time London tried to have certain testimony barred by physicians unless they were able to prove that the damage to Wilma's eyes was not aggravated during surgery after she arrived at the emergency room.

Doctors planned to testify that Wilma was suffering from a condition known as *phthisis bulbi*, or shrunken eyes, and the defense team thought that the impact of such testimony would be too prejudicial. Their objections were overruled.

London's witnesses were mainly there to testify that they had seen Johnnie on the day of the crime, and that he never had lamb chop sideburns. He did not explain the discrepancies in Johnnie's alibi that were exposed by Lawrence of the *Post-Dispatch*.

London moved for a direct acquittal after making his closing argument. The motion was denied, of course, since the only thing London had shown was that Wilma attributed some of Johnnie's features to Scar and vice versa.

It took the jury of two women and ten men less than an hour to reach a verdict. They found Johnnie guilty of robbery.

Since this was Johnnie's third felony conviction, he would receive a harsher sentence as provided by the Missouri Habitual Offenders Act. This meant that he faced a minimum of five years and a maximum of life imprisonment.

London told reporters after the verdict that he would file a motion for a new trial even though he had not fully determined the grounds. He planned to argue at sentencing that Johnnie could not receive more than 15 years imprisonment since that was the maximum he received at the first trial.

He was relying upon *North Carolina v. Pearce*, a 1969 U.S. Supreme Court decision holding that a defendant could not receive a longer combined sentence on appeal for the same offense than he did at the original trial. Doing so, the Court held, would effectively deprive a person of his right to appeal due to its "chilling" effect.

At the presentencing hearing on May 3, Judge Satz gave London and Fredericks nine days to file a memorandum regarding Johnnie's sentence. Was punishment limited to 15 years, which is what he received at the original trial on the robbery count, or could Johnnie receive to as much as 55 years, which is what he received on the assault charge?

London's position was clear.

Fredericks argued, however, that since Johnnie was convicted on the theory that the blinding was committed incidental to the robbery. As such, he could receive 55 years without violating the *Pearce* decision.

While the state charged him with two different offenses during the first trial, there was no law preventing them from reformulating the indictment to include the blinding as an ongoing part of the robbery.

On June 2, Judge Satz issued an opinion siding with the prosecution. He said that he planned to give Johnnie the same 55 years he received in the first trial. Satz based his decision on *State v. Johnson* (499 S.W. 371), where the Missouri Supreme Court held it was proper to combine two distinct felonies into a single charge where one felony was committed incidental to the other.

The blinding was committed for the sole purpose of preventing Wilma from identifying the robbers, and thus was part of the robbery.

Sheriffs returned Johnnie to Jefferson City where, barring a miracle, he would spend the rest of his life.

As expected, his defense team appealed the case. Their main arguments concerned the introduction of Scar's previous trial testimony and the constitutionality of his 55-year sentence. Other issues were raised, but they lacked serious merit.

Two teams of prosecutors penned the rebuttal brief. Preston Dean, Paul R. Otto, and John C. Danforth joined Ryan and Fredericks. (Danforth, by the way, later became governor of Missouri. His family owned the Ralston-Purina company).

While awaiting the appellate court's decision, Johnnie found a way to improve the public's perception of him. A Washington University graduate student began visiting the penitentiary in hopes of finding inmates interested in creating a "Scared Straight" type of program.

Jane Davis, who served on a panel studying juvenile justice, had spent time studying the program at Rahway State Prison. She met with a group of inmates at the Missouri Penitentiary in the fall of 1976 to discuss the idea of starting a program there.

At the first meeting, she asked several of the inmates to tell her something about how they ended up serving long terms. She began with the man sitting directly across from her.

"He puffed up like a proud peacock," she recalled, "looking me solidly and squarely in the eyes."

"Do you remember the Wilma Chestnut case?" he asked.

Davis was a month into her sophomore year when Wilma was blinded. "If I ever met that man," she said back then, "I would rip him apart."

"Yes," she said, "I remember it very well."

"Well," he said, "I'm Johnnie Lee Brooks."

She turned as red as a beet. She did not want to remain in the same room with him, let alone at the same table. She muttered something like "Your are?" or words to that effect. If he had intended to shock her, he had succeeded. She didn't know what else to say.

"Well," she said, "I'm glad that you want to help us save young men from ending up here like you."

Her religious faith helped her to restrain the anger she felt. After getting to know him, she concluded that he was the best candidate of the dozen or so volunteers.

He was selected chairman of the group calling itself the "Lifers" (they could not use the "Scared Straight" name for legal reasons).

She also felt that he affirmed a lesson from the gospel that even people who act "heinously among us" can be redeemed.

The Missouri Court of Appeals handed down its decision on February 22, 1977. The date marked, coincidentally, the second anniversary of Scar's imprisonment.

In an opinion running more than forty pages, the appellate court rejected all of Johnnie's arguments for reversal. There were no major procedural errors, evidentiary errors, or sentencing errors.

In its overview of the facts, the justices pointed out something the prosecution should have emphasized during each trial but neglected: "Ronnie Clower had never met either Harper or Craine."

So why would Ronnie – who had no criminal record – suddenly conspire with two complete strangers to rob someone who knew him?

The court also rejected London's argument that the prosecution deliberately misled the jury into believing that it would prove Johnnie assaulted Wilma. It accepted the state's reply that Earl's Fifth Amendment plea came as a surprise. Since London lacked evidence to the contrary, the argument lacked merit.

It agreed with London that Wilma's identification of Johnnie was problematic, but held that the jury had decided the issue in favor of the prosecution.

Regarding the core issues of the appeal – the reformulation of the robbery and the long sentence, the court concluded that both were permissible.

"We hold that evidence of the assault was admissible to show a consciousness of guilt or a desire to conceal the crime of robbery and prevent identification," the opinion stated.

"Such evidence would have been admissible even though the appellant was charged with robbery only, and it is therefore not material that he was charged with assault and robbery and the assault count was later dismissed."

Dissatisfied with the decision, Johnnie took his case to the Missouri Supreme Court. It was rejected. The United States Supreme Court also refused to review the case.

After the rejection of Johnnie's appeal, Wilma thought that she could finally put the fear of Johnnie being freed out of her mind.

Then a stranger came knocking.

Since no one was home with her except a 16-year-old friend, Wilma thought twice about answering the door. But when her friend said it was a white man dressed like a Catholic priest, she decided to answer it.

Who is it?" she said.

"It's Father Ralph Wright," the voice said.

"I'm a teacher at St. Abbey's and I've written a book about your case. It's in Braille. I would love to have you read it and get your opinion."

She opened the door and let him in.

"When he shook my hand," she recalled, "I was startled by how large his hands were. I figured that based on the size of his hands, he must have been a tall, muscular man who could easily have overpowered two small teenagers."

She pulled her hand away. She started reading the book.

It was called "Bearing False Witness."

As she read the first couple of pages, it became clear that the author believed Johnnie was innocent and also believed that Wilma had given false testimony in court.

"I don't know who you are, but don't ever come to my house again."

"May I leave the book?" he asked.

"No, you may not," Wilma snapped back.

"Very well, then," he said. "Thank you."

CHAPTER 16

Iceman Cometh

Father Wright returned a few weeks later. This time others were home, so Wilma opened the door.

"Hello, Wilma," he began. "I'm about to publish my book and was hoping that you would sign this statement saying that you have read it."

Wilma was furious.

"Do you think I'm a fool? I haven't read it and I never will. I asked you not to come back to my house."

When Colia found out about the two visits, she took Wilma to the St. Louis Priory School and went straight to the dean's office.

As they told him what happened, he expressed shock and dismay over Wright's behavior. "We had no idea that he was even working on the Johnnie Brooks case," he said. "I'll take the matter up with him right away. I assure you that this will never happen again."

The monk never visited her again.

Just as Father Wright had exhausted Wilma's patience, Johnnie was running out of options within the legal system.

Once he had exhausted appeals to state courts, he filed a petition for a writ of habeas corpus with the United States District Court for the Eastern District of Missouri. He filed it *pro se*, meaning that Johnnie was acting as his own lawyer.

Habeas corpus appeals were a cottage industry among inmates at the time. With no costs involved and no practical limits to the number of appeals that could be filed, prisoners with too much time on their hands churned out habeas corpus briefs in exchange for cigarettes, books, illicit acts and anything else in the prison bartering system.

While Johnnie's appeal made its way to the top of the pile, Drury and Father Wright continued to champion his cause on the outside. Drury mentioned Johnnie's plight from time to time in her *St. Louis Argus* column.

Even the *Globe-Democrat*, which used Johnnie as the poster boy for criminals beyond reformation, took note of his work to prevent juvenile delinquents from ending up where he was.

"Brooks said that if he had seen the prison in his youth," the story read, "he might have been different."

It noted that in addition to the crimes for which he was convicted, Johnnie had "numerous arrests on charges of assault and rape."

"These kids are what keeps homosexuality going in here," he said. "They can't protect themselves . . . This is the line of work I'd like to be in if I were out."

Warden Donald Wyrick praised Johnnie's work with Lifers, which had taken more than 500 delinquents through its five-hour program. "The feedback I get is that may juvenile officials feel it's a good approach," he said.

Two months later, Johnnie received the decision on his writ of habeas corpus.

In *Brooks v. Wyrick*, the federal court held that the state court acted properly in sentencing Johnnie to 55 years.

The decision noted that there were no new issues raised on appeal, and ruled that Johnnie's rights were not violated by using Scar's testimony from a previous trial. It also noted that the Supreme Court had refused to hear Johnnie's appeal.

Johnnie appealed to the United States Court of Appeals for the Eighth Circuit. On March 7, 1980, the court affirmed his conviction.

With that, Johnnie has exhausted all of his legal options.

He was 39 years old, and if he survived, he would not see freedom before age 75 at best.

He kept in touch with Father Wright, and Drury continued to visit periodically. His mother would come with Drury during the first three years of his incarceration, but she took ill in late 1978. She died in February of the following year. She was 56 years old.

Wilma's phone rang the day after Johnnie's mother passed away. To her dismay, it was none other than Father Wright.

"Hello," he said, "I just called to inform you that Mrs. Childs has died. She was the mother of Johnnie Brooks."

He waited for her response.

Wilma's words were slow in coming because she had never met Johnnie's mother, nor had she ever had any desire to meet her.

"Is he trying to lay some kind of guilt trip on me or what?" she wondered. She struggled to find words to say because she didn't want to be impolite.

"Well," she said, "everyone has to go sometime."

Father Wright was silent. "I just thought you'd want to know," he replied. "Good-bye."

He never called again.

Johnnie took her death hard, as he had dreamt of her living long enough to see him set free.

With that hope dashed, friends say that Johnnie struggled with depression. He took his insulin on schedule for a while after the last rejection of his case, but he started missing shots and neglecting his health by the summer of 1981.

That was the year Scar was released from the Missouri Penitentiary after serving 8 years of a twelve-year term, and the summer that Earl Harper died.

Earl, 25, was visiting a woman in the 4600 block on Kossuth on July 1 when he was fatally shot in the neck.

The woman he was visiting later told police that they were asleep when an armed intruder wearing a stocking mask climbed through the second story window of the woman's home between three and four o'clock in the morning.

A struggle ensued, she said, and Earl was shot in the face and neck, which proved fatal.

The intruder then forced the woman to walk down the street. When he saw an opening between two homes, he forced the woman inside and raped her. The woman said that he removed fifteen dollars from her purse after he escorted her home.

Police were not entirely convinced of the woman's story, so they asked her to take a polygraph test. The results were inconclusive.

Ironically, Earl had gone to Kingsbury with Johnnie to rape and rob Wilma. Johnnie could not have subdued Wilma without Earl's help. An even bigger irony: Earl was killed in the 4600 block of Kossuth. That was two blocks from the apartment building where Wilma, Laura, and Ronnie once lived (the 4400 block of Kossuth).

Tonya Freeman, the girl I had invited to live with me only to find out that she was writing to Johnnie, also died under bizarre circumstances.

In 1998, she had gotten involved with a drug addict named Randy Tanksley. They shared an apartment in the 5900 block of Theodore.

Tanksley had been purchasing his drugs from a 21-year-dealer named Jeffrey Jamison. Jamison was making a reputation for himself as a no non-sense dealer who would do anything to you if you didn't pay up.

Apparently Tanksley didn't believe him. He bought drugs from Jamison on credit and then failed to pay.

Shortly before midnight on April 23, neighbors saw Jamison enter Tonya's apartment. He found Tonya and Tanksley inside and threatened to kill them both unless Tanksley paid his debt.

Tonya begged him to give her until the next morning to get the money when the bank opened. She tried to get the money from relatives that night but no one had the cash. Jamison agreed.

When she returned from the bank, Tonya paid him and asked him to release Tanksley. Instead, Jamison ordered them to the kitchen, where he shot both of them in the head at point-blank range.

He was arrested several days later. He received two consecutive life sentences for the double homicide.

Johnnie was transferred to the newly opened Missouri Eastern Correctional Center in 1982. Located in Pacific, it was about two hours from the penitentiary and one hour from St. Louis. MECC was a medium security facility.

Although he was in a program that taught him how to repair watches, televisions, and other electronics, Johnnie must have known that it was merely something to keep him busy. Without new evidence, he had no chance of parole anytime soon.

By his second year at MECC, Johnnie started taking his insulin shots in a haphazard fashion. The chronic illnesses of juvenile diabetes were taking their toll. In early spring of 1985, medical personnel were concerned that if Johnnie didn't change, he stood a good chance of losing his feet.

Johnnie didn't seem to care. By late spring, he stopped taking insulin completely. His feet and legs turned gangrenous. By the end of June, doctors had no choice but to amputate both legs. Surgery was scheduled for June 30.

Jailers rushed him to St. John's Mercy Hospital in nearby Washington on Sunday morning after he complained of difficulty breathing. Chronic cigarette smoking, bronchitis and untreated diabetes finally caught up to him.

He died of cardiac arrest precipitated by bronchial distress shortly after arriving at the emergency room. He was 45 years old.

Like Earl, there was a certain irony in his death. Johnnie, who deprived Wilma of oxygen when he choked her, died from a lack of oxygen. Had he lived, he would have needed assistance getting around just as Wilma needs help getting around.

There are three major long-term symptoms of juvenile diabetes: the loss of limbs, cardiac arrest – and blindness.

CHAPTER 17

Second Wind

With Johnnie put away for good, Wilma continued moving forward in her private and academic life. She had several serious relationships in the middle 1970s, but the one man who seemed to keep coming back into mind was a professional musician named Edward C. Brown.

Everyone called him by his surname.

They met when she was fourteen. He treated her like a little sister, as he was four years older. Still, a girl at that age gets ideas, and she fantasized about being married to him one day.

The last time they met after years apart was a few months after she was blinded. She learned from friends that Brown traveled all over the country with the McPhersons, a local singing groups. The group of sisters hoped to become the female counterparts of the Jackson Five.

Brown also played piano in local clubs and for various gospel groups.

One day in 1974, Wilma got a call from Artis McCoy, her favorite uncle. "Uncie" attended Musick Baptist Church in Maryland Heights. (It was named in honor of Rev. Thomas Musick, a controversial Christian pioneer who once owned a plantation in the area.)

He said that the church had hired Brown as the organist and choir director a few months earlier. Wilma told Uncie to give Brown her phone number, which he did.

When he called, he told Wilma that he spent most of his time playing for a local jazz artist. He was living with a woman, he said, but he really wanted to see her.

Wilma agreed to dinner with him. It was clear from the first date that they had strong emotions for each other, but Wilma was adamant about not dating him until he was a free man.

He insisted that the relationship wasn't serious, but Wilma stood her ground. Brown moved out of the woman's house and moved in with a friend a few months later.

There was another problem. Brown's career suddenly took off. He spent the next several years traveling around the country. Wilma did not see him again until February 1978.

It was a bad time for Wilma. She had begun dating a man named Roosevelt in the intervening years. Roosevelt was murdered in November 1977. She ran into Brown by accident four months later.

They became inseparable.

On October 7, they were married at Musick before a standing-room-only congregation. The size of the crowd was due to media attention generated by the wedding announcement.

Their child was born in 1978. Wilma named her first and only child Eleasah Cushan Brown. They called her "Cush" for short.

Brown was often on the road during Cush's first year. It wasn't a problem because Wilma was so busy learning how to care for the baby and juggling other duties.

A point came, however, where it seemed that he was spending an extraordinary amount of time with a woman who was helping to promote his career.

The breaking point came when he told her that his mentor had adopted a child, and that he would be spending even more time away from home.

Wilma reminded him of his obligation to his own child who needed him at home just as much as someone else might need him elsewhere.

They struggled with the issue for the next year or so. When they could not work things out, she filed for divorce.

Unfortunately, the same media that blasted word of their marriage across the local news also discovered details of the divorce petition. News stories describing a stormy marriage followed.

Their divorce was finalized in June 1983.

While she was putting her life back together, she received a most unwelcome call.

A reporter wanted to know if the rumor was true: had Johnnie Brooks really offered to donate one of his eyes to her?

"I would never accept an eye from Johnnie Lee Brooks and let me tell you why," Wilma replied.

"Johnnie is an alcoholic and a drug abuser. Johnnie has diabetes. Those three things alone mean that his eyes are probably badly damaged."

"But you know what else? I would never accept an eye from Johnnie because I would be afraid of what I might see."

When Father Wright was asked about the offer, he confirmed that Johnnie had indeed made it.

"Johnnie wanted to give Wilma one of his eyes," he said, "so she would finally get a good look at his face and realize that he is not the person who blinded her."

Wilma thought Johnnie's timing was strange. Why had he chosen to offer her an eye after all these years? It turns out that he was ill. His diabetes was getting worse rapidly and his health was failing.

Besides, Johnnie knew full well that an orbital transplant was still unavailable. Wilma was his last, best, and only hope for getting out of prison.

The only way for him to get out with my help was for her to do what Father Wright suggested: call herself a liar and blame Johnnie's acts on Earnest Craine.

"There was no way in hell that I would do that," she said.

"What possible reason would I have to tell a lie like that? Why would I want to help the man who blinded me?"

Johnnie was soon transferred from the Missouri Penitentiary to a new facility in Pacific, Missouri, where they could better attend his medical needs. He was experiencing heart and circulatory problems.

By then, Colia was also having serious health problems. She had suffered from high blood pressure for years.

A kidney transplant and change of diet helped stabilize things, but she didn't have much to do except go to church and work. She and Mr. John Phillips remained friends, but they no longer dated or spent time together.

She lapsed into a coma in March 1986.

It was a devastating blow, Wilma said, because no one saw it coming. "She was living a normal life, not having any complaints when all of a sudden she's on her deathbed."

She was buried at Jefferson Barracks Cemetery next to Earnest Chestnut.

Wilma crawled into her shell for a while and just focused on sewing, working, and raising Cush.

She did eventually start dating again. He was a recovering drug addict who had been clean for six years. One day she attended a support group for the partners and families of recovering addicts.

As she stepped into the main meeting room, a male greeted her.
"Pat! How are you? What are you doing here?"

The voice sounded familiar but she couldn't quite place it.
"It's Ronnie," he said.
"Ronnie Clower?" she asked nervously.
"Yes!" he replied.
"Fine," she said, and then walked away.

She could not believe that he had the nerve to speak to her. She felt her blood pressure rising.

Wilma attended the meeting again two weeks later.

"I had often imagined a chance encounter with Ronnie," she said. "Now that the moment had arrived, questions I wanted to ask him raced through my mind."

She had asked herself for twenty years why Ronnie brought those people to her house.

"By the time I walked into the meeting that night, I had my message ready for him."

They asked first-time visitors to stand up, so people stood up one by one and told their stories. Each began the same way. "My name is _____, and I'm a drug addict."

When it was Wilma's turn, she said something a little different. Her friend said that Ronnie was sitting directly across the circle from her. She stood up and recited a memorized speech:

Second Wind

My name is Wilma Chestnut, and I'm the victim of a drug addict. The person who victimized me is in this room tonight, but I'm not going to mention him by name.

All I want to do is ask him some questions.

Why did you bring those people to my house that day? I really can't understand why you brought Johnnie to my house. You knew he was an addict and you knew he had hurt other women in the past.

I trusted you.

I thought you were my friend. I trusted you, and you brought someone to my house who you should have known would hurt me.

I trusted you because my friend loved and trusted you. I let my guard down for a minute, and for that I was blinded the rest of my life."

"I could feel myself becoming emotional as the words poured out of me," she said.

"I had never really given myself time to grieve over what happened. I was in shock after the incident, and by the time I recovered, I was too busy trying to reorder my life to really focus on why those men chose to hurt me like that."

"I really would like to hear your response," she said at the end, "but I won't identify you. I'm leaving my phone number on the desk with the counselor tonight. I hope you will call me."

She didn't have to identify him because everyone knew who she was talking about. They knew because Ronnie looked down at the floor while she spoke, and he got up and left the meeting as soon as she finished.

One day long after that, Wilma felt ill.

She had Cush take her to the emergency room at St. Mary's Hospital. Cush asked if it would be okay if she went to the employment office there while Wilma waited to see a doctor. She told her to go ahead.

When she came back, she was giggling and said that she ran into this really cute guy that she had given her phone number recently when they met at the bus stop.

"Oh, really," Wilma said. "What's his name?

"He told me his name was Ronald Cook," Cush answered. "But he put his name down as "Ronald Clower Jr. on the job application."

Wilma nearly fainted.

"Cush," she said sternly, you tell that boy to come here right now!"

When the boy came over and sat beside her, Wilma could barely hold her rage.

"Do you know who I am?"

"Yes, ma'am," he said. "But I didn't know you were Cush's mother until just now."

"Do you know that your daddy is part of the reason that I'm blind?" I asked.

"I know, Ms. Chestnut, and I'm really sorry," he said.

"That's why I use my mother's maiden name, because everywhere I go, people want to know if I'm the same person who hurt you."

She was a bit embarrassed for putting him on the spot that way, she said, "but the thought of Ronnie's son being in my house or with my daughter made me sick at the stomach."

"Listen, child," she said as she touched him. "That was way before you were even born, so nobody's blaming you for what happened."

He thanked her, left the hospital and went on his way.

When the doctors asked about her symptoms, Wilma mentioned that she felt tired most of the time. Their next question was whether she exercised or played any sports.

"A light bulb went off in my head."

She had been such a tomboy when she was young. She challenged boys to races and played baseball with boys because girls acted like they never heard of the sport.

She once harbored dreams of being a gymnastics instructor. But ten years after Cush was born, she had put on weight around the middle.

That's when she remembered Sonny, the brother of Uncie's wife, Laverne. Sonny was the one who encouraged her to study karate in 1972 after she recovered.

He also encouraged her to resume playing the sports that she enjoyed as a child. She soon discovered that many semi-professional sports activities were available for people with disabilities.

Some of them were devoted exclusively to the vision-impaired.

Sonny told her to try weightlifting. It was great strength training, he said, but it was also something at which she might excel since she was so active in other sports.

She had always regarded weightlifting as a sport for men. Sonny took her to a few competitions that were exclusively for women to show her how wrong she was.

The sport had changed tremendously in the past 30 years, he said, and there were new opportunities ever since Arnold Schwarzenegger made the sport respectable.

Once again, Sonny became her primary coach. She started slowly, doing repetitions with 30 and then 40 and then 50 pounds. Once she felt that she could lift more without injuring herself, she doubled those amounts.

People were so impressed with her natural athletic abilities that they encourage her to enter state and national competitions.

Less than a year after taking up the sport, she had broken all state records for weightlifting. The leagues were comprised of vision-impaired athletes, but they were often high school and college jocks who lost their vision just as unexpectedly as Wilma lost her own.

In the summer of 1987, she traveled to Albuquerque to compete in the 11th annual competition sponsored by the United State Association of Blind Athletes, or USABA.

There were over 500 competitors, which was one third of the nation's total. On the last day the squats competition, she successfully lifted 160 pounds.

It was a new record and twelve pounds more than when she broke the previous record a year earlier. Her weight was down to 132 pounds at the time.

In April 1990, the annual competition was held in Riverdale, California. After a weekend of grueling contests, Wilma was crowned best female power lifter in the USABA.

CHAPTER 18

Blessed

Thanks primarily to the generosity of St. Louisans (though donations came in from every corner of the globe), Wilma was able to live on the proceeds of the Wilma Chestnut Fund for nearly 30 years.

It not only paid for the home that she still lives in, but it paid the annual taxes every year so she did not have to worry about losing it. She was able to pay college fees and pay for Cush to take ballet lessons and other activities.

"To all those little children, paperboys, and inmates who apologized for sending a "meager" donation of a few pennies," she said, "please know that all those pennies put together were big enough to meet most of my living expenses for three decades."

In addition to the fund, new laws were passed to help disabled Americans become entrepreneurs.

This gave Wilma an opportunity to start her own business.

Using the Randolph-Sheppard Act in conjunction with working with the National Association for the Blind, she applied for a program that taught visually impaired Americans to undergo training to operate their own businesses.

Under the act, the blind were given priority to any vacant store properties inside all federal buildings. The sole exception was Veterans Affairs buildings, where disabled veterans received top priority.

Wilma has always loved to cook. She thought that if she was unable to become an artist, she could open a restaurant or a convenience store that sold meals-to-go.

In the late 1990s, as inflation and expenses finally took their toll on the Wilma Chestnut Fund, she received computer instruction from an on-the-job training program hosted by Goodwill Industries.

Each student was required to submit a mock business proposal.

"Since I loved cooking, I asked my classmates to bring in a family recipe or a personal favorite recipe," she said.

"Everyone contributed at least one and some brought several."

Wilma typed up all the recipes and published them in a booklet. They gave it the suggestive title of "Messin' Around in the Kitchen," and an artist who worked in the building drew cover art consisting of an attractive lady cooking in her kitchen.

Each student brought one prepared dish for a special luncheon to promote the booklet. The instructor was highly impressed.

"We sold every copy. I passed the course with flying colors, but now I had even bigger ideas."

She kept collecting recipes for the next few years. She remembered her days at the Missouri School for the Blind where they learned how to use kitchen appliances, but where there was little instruction on actually preparing anything but the most basic meals.

Her plan was to publish a cookbook designed for visually impaired cooks, but with recipes that would interest everyone.

She had learned secret family recipes over the years. Now that she was traveling to New Orleans every year to visit her father and extended family during Mardi Gras, she had tripled the number of recipes in her repertoire.

Wilma remarried in April 1990 after a whirlwind courtship. Her husband had a troubled past, like many young black men, but he was a good partner and a good stepfather to Cush.

Blessed

After being accepted into the Lions Club's Business Opportunities for Missouri's Blind, Wilma went to Jefferson City for six months of training in February 2003. Eric remained home with Cush.

He was coming home from work in July using his normal route. As he reached the top of a hill and crossed, a police cruiser heading to an emergency slammed into his car. He died at the hospital a few hours later.

Berkeley County police later claimed that Eric had drugs in his blood stream.

"I had no way of disproving that," she said.

"Eric dabbled in marijuana from time to time like a lot of men his age. But I don't think he was under the influence that evening."

Witnesses said that the cruiser came through the intersection at an excessive rate of speed.

Wilma took time to mourn her loss, but she was right in the middle of the training program and could not afford to drop out. She finished the course on schedule and began scouting possible locations for a business.

The program offered four levels of degrees.

The first was the most basic. It allowed the owner to clean and refill vending machines along with cleaning break areas. Level Two allowed the person to run a store as long as there was no cooking. Level Three licensees could run a snack shop with self-service microwave machines. They could also cook on a grill.

Level Four gave the owner full cafeteria privileges.

Wilma received a Level 4 certificate but when the next set of stores were open for bidding, the only thing available was a Level 2 shop. She reluctantly bid on a shop in the Robert A. Young Federal Building and won.

She named the store Aboragani. The grand opening was announced with big stories in the local media.

A competitor downstairs constantly bragged to her that no one could beat his weekly income of $800. She said nothing to him about it, but she surpassed that amount within a couple of months.

Wilma had so much space that she submitted a redesign plan that included a kitchen for serving hot meals. Unfortunately, she got ahead of herself while the plan was pending.

She started serving hot soup and offering special Friday lunches. She prepared the food at home and Cush helped her bring it to work.

They warmed the food on a small grill. Cush was her business partner and supervisor of the makeshift kitchen. They were clearing $2500 a month within six months.

They had a magazine rack near the dining area. Newspapers, magazines and other literature were available. Wilma allowed people to donate any literature they wanted as long as it wasn't pornography, racially offensive or otherwise indecent or inappropriate.

An Army woman came in from time to time and left a stack of *Final Call* newspapers.

A white customer took exception to her having the paper in the shop. When she said that she found it offensive, Wilma had Cush remove all copies of the *Final Call* from the shelf and stick them in a well-ventilated area between two vending machines.

She planned to keep them there until the woman who donated them returned, which was usually once or twice a month.

Before she returned, the complainant came back. She noticed a man remove one of the papers from the stack and start to read it.

The next thing Wilma knew, the board was threatening to revoke her license for serving hot meals in violation of her contract. Customers were ready to form a picket outside the building when they heard about it.

Cush wanted to fight the revocation, but Wilma said no.

She reminded her of a simple lesson: don't fight someone over something that isn't yours in the first place.

"The store did not belong to me," she said. "It belonged to the government and I was operating at its discretion and under its guidelines." The store was shut down and later awarded to someone else.

They mourned the loss of Aboragani as though they had lost a family member, but again, Wilma did not dwell on it.

"There is always something worse than what you are going through to put your own troubles in perspective."

Six months after the store closed, Hurricane Katrina wiped out centuries of New Orleans history and killed thousands. Wilma lost family members, but some of them managed to survive and to get in touch with her.

She had more than two dozen relatives crowded into her three-bedroom home within a month. People slept everywhere.

As news reports mentioned their plight, neighbors and friends allowed some to move in with them for a long as need be.

Thankfully, many were able to find employment in the St. Louis area, while others chose to return to New Orleans.

Wilma's father survived Katrina.

She still visits him each March to celebrate Mardi Gras with the Zulu Social Aid and Pleasure Club. He was governor of the Zulus in 1999 and 2000.

With lessons learned from the first store, Wilma applied for a license last year to run a janitorial service in another government building. Her business plan was approved and now she's waiting for the financing. She is optimistic that everything will work out.

"In an interview a few years ago," she said, "a reporter asked me about my legacy. I told him that I wasn't sure what it would be, but that I had a very simple message for anyone who was interested in my life story."

When she was first blinded, she felt like God had failed her and no one was there for her when she needed them most.

But after the outpouring of love she received in months and years after the attack, she came to another conclusion.

"God was there for me, and He has always been there for me. It took the people of St. Louis and their faith in humanity to remind me of that. Their dedication renewed my own faith and gave a second wind, a new life."

Being blind did not deter Wilma from competing in the Miss Black St. Louis Pageant – or anything else.

**Wilma married Edward C. Brown – a musician
and her childhood sweetheart – in October 1978.**

Wilma is given away by her favorite uncle to Eddie Brown.

A pensive moment with her first and only child, Eleasah.

Colia and Wilma attend Cush's graduation from kindergarten.

The heinous crime against Wilma made headlines over a five-year period.

**Wilma and her second husband, Eric House, capture
moments from their wedding in the spring of 1990.**

New Mexico

Blind woman sets lifting mark

ALBUQUERQUE — A woman broke her own record by lifting 160 pounds in a powerlifting event at the 11th annual national games of the United States Association of Blind Athletes.

Wilma Chestnut, who weighs 132 pounds, on Sunday broke her powerlifting record of 148 pounds set at the games last year. Chestnut's 160-pound lift came in the squats event.

Chestnut, 33, was blinded when she was 18 by a robber who wanted to prevent her from being able to identify him.

Chestnut and about 500 other blind athletes will compete through Saturday in the games sponsored by the Albuquerque chapter of the USABA at the University of New Mexico. Other events are gymnastics, cycling, judo, wrestling, swimming and track and field.

Chestnut said blind athletes train and compete pretty much the same as sighted competitors.

"We've got just about everything they've got," she said.

Nearly 15,000 blind athletes belong to USABA. New Mexico's two chapters have about 100 members.

Staff and Wire Reports

In addition to karate, Wilma also embraced weightlifting, track, and beep-ball, a form of baseball for the visually-impaired.

Wilma sits at a specially-designed cash register while Cush and granddaughter Uriah relay details of a proposed lunch menu for Aboragani, their convenience store.

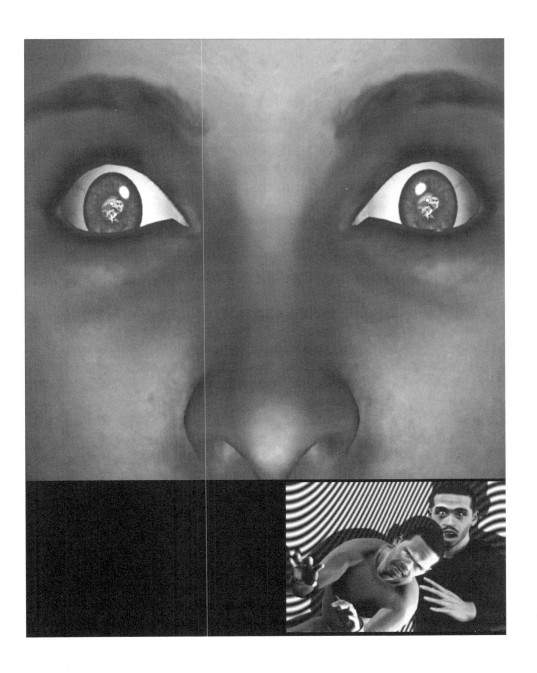

Artist's conception of the last thing Wilma ever saw before losing consciousness: the face of the man choking her and of the man trying to stop him. She was blind when she awoke.

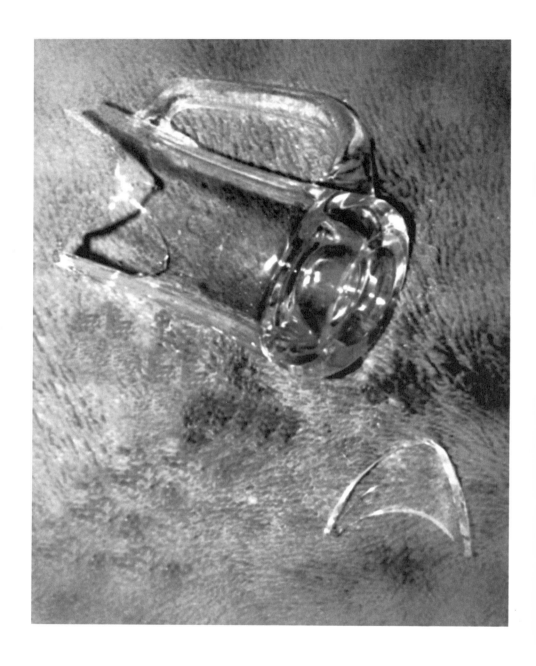

**Her attacker broke a glass mug similar to this
one, and then used a shard to "cut her eyes out."**

METROPOLITAN POLICE DEPARTMENT – CITY OF ST. ?UIS
HOLDOVER SICK AND INJURY REPORT

72-134710

☐ Original Report ☒ Supplementary Report

RECORDS SECTION
File Copy
☒ Station

File No. For Records Section
Complaint No. 185317

☐ Assignment Received by ☐ Radio ☒ Station

Date 9-30-'71 Time 4:12 P.M. Assignment Received

Concerning Assault/w/I/to do G/B/H 1. Original C.R. 184611 5. District Report 4 Date of this Report 9-30-'71

Date and Time of Arrest 9-19-71 2:15 P.M. 6. Place of Arrest 3857 KENNERLY 7. District 7 8. Location Code

Prisoner BROOKS, JOHNNIE LEE 10. Home Address 3857 KENNERLY 11. Business Address 18600 ST CHARLES

Pedigree Race N Sex M Age 30 Date of Birth 10-3-40 Marital Status S e of Birth 7135 Occupation LABORER

Arrest Register Number 7-3196 14. Arrest Report Complaint Number 184611

Charge ASSAULT w/I to do G.B.H. – STEALING O/5 – PAROLE VIOLATION

Officer Assigned to Holdover Notified of Illness or Injury TKY BELL Rank Name DSN 137 Time 4:00 A.M. Date 9-30-71

17. Alleged Illness or Injury DIABETIC

18. Prisoner Removed from Cell No. 16 by TKY Rank BELL Name DSN 137 Time 4:35 A.M. Date 9-30-71

19. Prisoner Conveyed to City Hospital No. 1 Via Car 417 by Ptn John UNDERSINGER 9435 and Ptn Kevin Condon 5660

Examined by Dr. BERNABE 21. Diagnosis DIABETES

☐ Admitted Dis Ward Custody of

☒ Returned to Holdover Via Car 417 by Ptn John UNDERSINGER 9435 Kevin Condon 5660

Prisoner Turned Over to the Custody of TKY. BELL Rank Name DSN 137 and Placed in Cell No. 13

Units Notified by Last Name

Narrative If Required:

Reporting Officer Ptn Kevin Condon 5760 304 4A4

Approving Officer Sergt Thomas J. Murphy

Asked whether he had seen a police report confirming
Johnnie's claim of being hospitalized while in custody on
September 23, 1971, the monk finally admitted that he had
not. Actual report proves that Johnnie was not treated until
the following week – after his arrest for blinding Wilma.

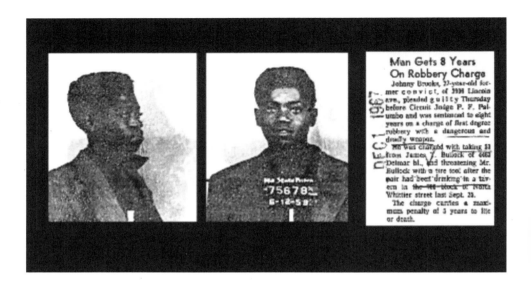

`·75678·`
`6-18-59`

Johnnie was the only suspect who had prior arrests for assault, robbery, and rape. He went to prison in 1959 after using a firearm to rob a man of a quarter. He tried to kill the officer chasing him after the robbery. He used a knife to rob a man in 1970. A year later, he asked Ronnie for a knife to rob Wilma.

MO. DEPT. OF CORRECTIONS
14682

```
 1        A   I had put ?omie in the bed, I believe, and I

 2   had Daphne with me.

 3        Q   How about Herbert, was he there at any time

 4   those young men were there?

 5        A   Yes, he came while they were there.

 6        Q   About what time did Herbert get home?

 7        A   About ten after twelve.

 8        Q   This is the five-year-old?

 9        A   No.

10        Q   How old was he?            A   Herbert was

11   about eight or nine.

12        Q   Eight or nine?            A   Yes.

13        Q   Did you give Herbert anything?

14        A   I gave him a dime.

15        Q   Did he have lunch there at the apartment with

16   you?                    A   I don't think he ate lunch.  I

17   don't remember.

18        Q   After you gave him the dime, did he stay there?

19        A   He went across the street to the candy lady.

20        Q   Did you see him any more that day?

21        A   Yes, he came back home after he left the candy

22   lady.

23        Q   After he left the candy lady he came back home?

24        A   Yes.

25        Q   When he came back to the apartment after he left
```

173

Though never revealed during Johnnie's trials, there was a secret witness who identified him as the man seen inside the apartment at noon and seen leaving just before three o'clock.

Governor: Wilma poses with her father, Curtis Woolridge, at a 2007 Mardi Gras celebration. Woolridge was twice elected governor of the Zulu Social Aid and Pleasure Club.

Intruder kills man, rapes woman

A 25-year-old Northwoods man was killed and a 29-year-old woman raped early Wednesday by an armed intruder who climbed through a window of the woman's home on the North Side.

Earl Harper, of 6842 Pasadena Blvd., was shot to death about 3:25 a.m during a struggle with an intruder armed with a pistol and wearing a stocking mask, according to city police.

Harper was pronounced dead at City Hospital.

The woman, whom Harper was visiting, told police that when she awakened she saw Harper and the intruder struggling. The intruder then shot Harper in the face and neck and forced the woman to walk down the street, where he raped her between two houses, she told police.

The woman told Ruskin Avenue District police that the man then walked her back to the house, robbed her of $15 and fled.

Crime roundup

early-morning telephone calls.

The request appeared in Tuesday's Globe-Democrat.

Detective Sgt. John Siebenman, supervisor of the Hampton Avenue District detective bureau, said there has been "a rash of burglaries" in the area bounded by Chippewa and Eichelberger streets, Kingshighway Boulevard and Hampton Avenue, apparently committed by people who first call to make sure no one is at home. A police officer who lives in the 5300 block of Itaska Street received two such phone calls Wednesday morning, Siebenman said.

The telephone number of the Hampton Avenue District is 444-5421.

● Two men have been charged and

advisement because of problems with the victim's identification of the suspects, according to an assistant circuit attorney.

Ruskin Avenue District officers responded to the burglary call at 3:05 a.m. at 5461 Robin Ave. Katie Davis, 23, said three young males entered through the window and took a typewriter, electric piano and television, with a total estimated value of $340.

Officers Clifford Robbins, Thomas Schulte and Roy Simmons arrested the three suspects a short time later in the 5300 block of Harney Avenue. The typewriter was found in the victim's back yard. The piano and television were not recovered.

● A fuse for an M-60 land mine was recovered in the back yard of a home at 4718 St. Louis Ave. Wednesday morning after police received an anonymous telephone call.

Bomb and arson Detective Ronald Lingle

Johnnie Brooks Dies In Prison; Robber Blinded Victim In '71

Johnnie Lee Brooks, convicted in the highly publicized robbery and blinding of Wilma Chestnut in 1971, died Sunday morning after suffering what appeared to be a heart attack at the Missouri Eastern Correctional Center in Pacific.

Spokesmen for the prison and St. John's Mercy Hospital in Washington, Mo., confirmed Brooks' death but refused to disclose additional information.

Barbara Drury, known as the "Jailhouse Angel" for her work with prison inmates, said she had learned of Brooks' death from a fellow inmate. Drury said he had suffered from diabetes and had repeatedly refused to take insulin for the disease. He was 45.

She said Brooks had worked repairing watches and television sets at the

Pacific prison, where he had been held for the past three years. Before that, he was at the Missouri Penitentiary in Jefferson City.

The 1971 case drew national attention. Chestnut was 17 at the time; she was robbed while baby-sitting at an aunt's apartment, then blinded to prevent her from identifying her assailant. Brooks was convicted in 1972 and was sentenced to 15 years in prison for robbery and 55 years for assault.

An appeals court overturned the conviction. In April 1975, Brooks was found guilty only on the robbery charge after a Supreme Court ruling on double jeopardy indicated that Brooks could be tried on only one charge in the incident.

Brooks had maintained that another man had blinded Chestnut.

Some call it karma: Earl Harper, the boy who assisted Johnnie in the choking, robbery and planned rape of Wilma Chestnut, was killed in 1981 at a girlfriend's home. She was allegedly raped after he was fatally shot – in the neck.

Johnnie died in prison in 1985. The cause of death involved two of the three long-term complications of juvenile diabetes: cardiac arrest and loss of limbs. The third effect: blindness.

Chapter 19

Common Sense

One of Johnnie's attorneys told me that the name of the person who actually blinded Wilma Chestnut would remain a mystery for the ages. I disagreed.

It doesn't take the genius of Einstein or curiosity of George Washington Carver to figure out who blinded Wilma. All it takes is common sense and deductive reasoning.

Johnnie's criminal record reveals a social deviant with no sense of proportion. He would just as soon kill you for three dollars as he would for $30 or $3,000. He would do anything to feed his alcoholism.

Secondly, he was a career criminal. As with most repeat offenders, Johnnie developed a *modus operandi*, or method of operation.

So did Scar. Scar's weakness, for example, was vending machines. He discovered early in his criminal career that there were ways to outsmart vending machines, particularly the ones made in the primitive years – the 1950s and 1960s.

With some machines, all you had to do was wait until the shopkeeper turned his head or walked twenty or thirty feet from the machine, then take a screwdriver and stick it into the lock's keyhole.

Hit the lock with a hammer or something heavy. The lock would pop and you had access to the coins.

Scar was arrested more than a dozen times for breaking into vending machines. He clearly assumed that he was good at it, and maybe he was. Maybe he was caught a dozen times out of 50 or 100 or 200 break-ins.

Once a recidivist figures out how to commit an offense without getting caught, he tends to stick to the same method or an improved method.

If a criminal is not too bright, however, he will use the same technique that got him caught earlier. He will assume that his capture was caused by circumstance and not technique.

Thus, when Johnnie robbed a man for a quarter at gunpoint in 1959, he had not counted on a police officer showing up in the middle of the crime. The odds of that happening twice were a million to one.

When he robbed another man for ten dollars and a cheap watch seven years later, he used the same technique: run up to someone, put him in fear of losing his life, take the money and run.

The reason Johnnie claimed that he had always admitted guilt in the past is that he was usually caught red-handed. It had nothing to do with him having a conscience.

Three men were involved in robbing Wilma.

The prosecution argued that the three conspirators were Johnnie, Earl and Scar.

The defense claimed that the three were Ronnie, Earl and Scar. An examination of the criminal records of the four men is instructive regarding who were the likely perpetrators.

The following chart is a perfect place to start.

Criminal Histories of Suspects

CHARGE	Johnnie	Earl	Earnest	Ronnie
*Rape/ Sodomy	3	0	0	0
* Robbery	6	1**	1**	0
Burglary (building)	1	1	0	0
Burglary (machine)	0	0	5	0
Theft	1	0	4	0
DUI/DWI	2	0	1	0
Marijuana	0	0	3	0
Weapon	3	0	1	0

* Crimes against a person.
** Victim: Wilma Chestnut

Ronald Clower Sr. had no felony convictions at the time of the attack or when this research concluded in April 2011.

A few notes about this chart. Some criminal charges typically go hand in hand. Crime statistics show that a man who rapes a woman will usually commit sodomy, so you often see both two charges on arrest records or indictments. The same is true of burglary of machines and theft.

TYPES OF CRIME

Criminologists, sociologists and related professions have determined that nearly all crimes fall into three broad categories: (1) crimes against another person; (2) crimes against property; (3) victimless crimes or crimes of self-victimization.

1. Assault is the most typical crime against another person. It is a pre-requisite for most other crimes against a person – robbery, rape and homicide for example.

2. Property crimes include vandalism, burglary, theft, forgery and similar offenses.

3. The third category of crimes includes prostitution, public intoxication and drug abuse.

Based solely upon the chart above, which includes most arrests and con-victions for the four people allegedly involved in robbing and blinding Wilma, it is obvious from a statistical standpoint that Ronnie was the *least likely* person to be involved.

Not only did he lack an arrest record, but he was the only person in the group who knew Wilma.

He was also the only person in the group who only knew one other sus-pect. Ronnie knew Johnnie, but had never met Earl or Scar before September 23, 1971.

Similarly, Scar was only vaguely familiar with Johnnie and Earl, the reason being that he lived in Austin, Texas. He visited his sister in St. Louis periodically, and she happened to live across the street from Earl and Johnnie.

The *common denominator* in the group is Johnnie. He was the only person who knew the other three.

This brings up another point, the issue of proximity. Here are the addresses of the four alleged suspects on September 23, the day that Wilma was blinded.

Ronnie Clower: 4601 Enright Avenue   (4.2 miles from Johnnie)
                   4418 Kossuth Avenue (1.8 miles from Johnnie)

Earl S. Harper: 3855 Kennerly Avenue
Earnest C. Craine: 3856 Kennerly Avenue (directly across the street)
Johnnie L. Brooks: 3857 Kennerly Avenue (next door to Earl)

With the exception of Scar, the four suspects lived at home with their mothers most of the time. Ronnie's mother lived on Enright, but he spent time at a house on Kossuth.

Wilma said that the man who introduced himself as Johnnie bragged about hanging out near the intersection of Vandeventer and St. Ferdinand.

Arrest records and news reports show that Johnnie once resided at 3906 Lincoln Avenue. That's only one block over from Kennerly. In addition, that intersection is only three blocks from Johnnie's former apartment on Lincoln.

Scar would not have given her that detail since he lived out of state.

Wilma never said that the man who attacked her had broad shoulders. This was another instance where Father Wright – and later Johnnie's lawyers – took her statement out of context.

She said repeatedly that the man who attacked her *had his shirt open* at the top, which made him *appear* to have broad shoulders and a slim waist.

The mug shot taken of Johnnie on September 15 shows him wearing his shirt the way he did routinely. It was unbuttoned down to his navel.

MOTIVE MEANS and OPPORTUNITY

MOBILITY

1. Earl did not have a car or access to a car.
2. Scar did not have a car or access to a car.
3. Ronnie did not have a car or access to a car.
4. *Johnnie* had a car and access to a car on the day of the crime.

MOTIVE

Johnnie borrowed money on Wednesday that he promised to *repay by Friday*. He was a habitual smoker and drinker, and he had to borrow money to support both habits. He needed parts for his car and he needed gas. He repeatedly talks about borrowing money for all three in his statement to Father Wright.

As indicated, Johnnie would rob you and put your life in jeopardy for any amount. He needed at least two dollars by Friday to repay Sammie. He stole a used tape recorder and a twenty-dollar stereo from Wilma and took them to the pawn shop on *Thursday*.

MEANS

1. No one saw Ronnie with a weapon or heard him ask for one on September 23.
2. No one saw Earl with a weapon or heard him ask for one on September 23.
3. Johnnie is the only person who claims to have heard Scar ask Ronnie for a weapon on September 23.
4. Ronnie testified under oath several times that *Johnnie asked him for a knife on the day of the crime*, and that he gave him one. That's why

Ronnie's mother became hysterical when she saw him go downstairs to Johnnie's car. She thought that he was going to join them and sensed a bad result. That's why they call it "mother's intuition."

II. Types of Crime

b) Johnnie was the only suspect who had a history of armed robbery.

c.) Johnnie was the only one who had used a knife in the past to commit a crime.

OPPORTUNITY

By his own admission, Scar was alone with Wilma for approximately twenty minutes. He made no attempt to touch her or harm her in any way. In fact, he left the apartment because he grew tired of waiting for Johnnie and Earl to return.

Earl, Scar and Wilma all testified that Johnnie was the person who choked her.

Johnnie was the only person with Wilma *after* the items were stolen. He specifically asked for time alone with her because he planned to rape her *and* to do something so she would not be able to identify them.

d.) Johnnie was the only one of four suspects who had been arrested for rape before September 23. He was also arrested at least twice for oral sodomy. None of the others were ever convicted on similar charges.

e.) When Wilma was in the hospital, nurses informed her that a woman on another floor had identified Johnnie as the man who raped her and then sodomized her.

Neither was Wilma sure about the scar on her assailant's face. She said at the deposition and at the first trial that he *might* have had a scar on his lip but she wasn't sure.

The worst thing about the whole "she nailed the wrong guy" business is that Father Wright recognized from the very beginning that Wilma was not sure about the facial features of either Johnnie or Scar.

It was obvious that she conflated their features. Wright used this information to try to discredit Wilma.

Johnnie fit the classic definition of chutzpah. The classic illustration of chutzpah is the boy charged with killing his parents asking the judge for mercy because he was an orphan.

Johnnie blinded Wilma, then had the audacity to demand acquittal because she could not pick him out of a photo lineup.

The only way to understand why Wilma confused some of Johnnie's physical characteristics with those of Scar is to read Scar's account of what happened.

Father Wright and others came to the conclusion that Wilma committed perjury, but they had not even heard Scar's testimony before arriving at such a scurrilous conclusion.

By the time they heard Scar's account, they were too far invested in Johnnie's alibi to admit that they were wrong.

Because Wilma thought that she was dying as she gasped for breath and her vision became clouded, the last image her eyes captured was the face of the man trying to kill her, and directly behind him, the face of the man trying to save her.

They say that your entire life flashes before your eyes in the moments before you die or think that you are dying. So no one should be surprised that Wilma's identification testimony was inconsistent.

To compound matters, Wilma awoke to find that she could no longer see. Who among us, faced with this realization, would have done any better at recalling details of an attack when we now have to cope with being blind?

Any priest callous enough to go to a crime victim's house – one blinded by her attacker no less – and ask her to sign a statement calling herself a perjurer needs to have his head, and his heart, examined.

Father Wright may have been a good Benedictine monk, but he was certainly no Adrian Monk.

In his unchecked zeal, Wright deluded others who trusted his research and judgment into thinking that Johnnie was the victim and Wilma was the criminal.

Father Wright offered me a copy of Johnnie's statement of October 28, the one where he exhibits extraordinary recall of one supposedly ordinary date in his life, because he thought it would convince me of Johnnie's innocence.

He also provided me with a portion of Johnnie's diary.

But he failed to provide me with a most important piece of information: the police report of September 23.

In all of his journals, Father Wright never mentions the police report confirming Johnnie's visit to the hospital while in custody on September 23.

He did not provide it or mention it because it never existed. What does exist is a report from September 30, a full week after the crime.

––––––––––––

Why didn't Johnnie's lawyer's surprise the jury by calling in the pawn shop clerks who accepted the stolen record player and tape recorder? Who would the pawn brokers have identified as the seller?

––––––––––––

Earl said that he secretly called the police that same day and told them that he had information about the attack on Wilma Chestnut.

Earl's participation raises another element of Johnnie's modus operandi. Johnnie started to include at least one juvenile when he worked with accomplices.

That way, if anyone was accused or arrested after the fact, the juvenile could take the fall. He would face charges in juvenile court, which was usually nothing more than a slap on the wrist or a few months in a Boys Town correctional facility.

Johnnie used a juvenile when he stripped cars after his release from prison in 1969, and he used Earl as a potential shield when they robbed Wilma.

Earl was willing to take the rap for robbery since he was a juvenile. Johnnie canceled the deal, however, when he committed crimes that were not part of the bargain.

Johnnie needed alcohol to provide the courage he lacked when sober. He had a few drinks before he robbed the man in the bar after stalking him, and he left Wilma's house to get a bottle of beer before he blinded her and tried to rape her.

Contrary to his confessions to Father Wright, Johnnie never took responsibility for his crimes unless caught red-handed.

      a.) He took the Fifth Amendment in 1970 incidental to the car-stripping arrest.

      b.) He pleaded the Fifth Amendment when police arrested him on September 29 for blinding Wilma

      c.) He exercised the right to remain silent at each and every trial.

He was caught with the man's watch in his pocket seconds after the YMCA robbery, so he couldn't very well claim that he was not guilty.

He was identified by the bar owner and the victim from mug shots the day after the bar robbery where he stalked his victim.

Since Johnnie was a regular at the bar, which was around the corner from his mother's house on Lincoln Avenue, he would be hard pressed to claim mistaken identity.

Rape and Sodomy

Johnnie forcibly performed oral sodomy on a woman whose home he broke into and threatened to kill in 1971. Although he was arrested, the woman was too ashamed to testify against him because she knew that his lawyers would blame her, a typical stunt in those days when people regarded rape victims as someone "just asking for it."

He came back to the car after blinding Wilma and bragged about how he [raped her, yet police found no semen or other evidence that she was sexually violated. The only proof that he touched her below the waist was her missing panties. He took them but dropped the souvenir of proof on the way out of the building.

This is pure speculation, but perhaps his violence against women had to do with sexual performance issues.

Neither Earl, Scar or Ronnie was ever arrested on rape charges.

Scar and Johnnie were the only two with long rap sheets. Johnnie had been arrested more than once for rape and sodomy; Scar had never been arrested for any *crimes against women* – or men, for that matter.

His record is almost uniformly burglaries and public intoxication. Nearly *all of Johnnie's crimes* involved putting someone's life in jeopardy for a few dollars.

The Secret Witness

Finally, there was Herbert. Herbert was the little boy mentioned early in the book, the one who represents the unanticipated snag in every serious crime.

Johnnie calculated that he had about three hours to rob and rape Wilma. What he had not anticipated was someone stopping by during that time.

Herbert came home for lunch. He saw three men in the apartment with Wilma, who was cleaning the bathroom.

Wilma gave him a dime after he ate lunch, then sent him back to school.

Johnnie had blinded Wilma by 2:45 that afternoon and was about to rape her.

However, he could hear the voices of school children from the street below. He panicked, grabbed Wilma's panties as a souvenir, and then headed for the rear of the building.

A little boy saw him as he made his escape, the same little boy who had seen him inside the apartment at noon.

When police questioned Herbert about the visitors, he initially said that he could identify them.

Upon being shown mug shots, Herbert quickly identified Johnnie as the man he saw in the apartment at midday and the one he saw leaving just after the school day.

160

"I got scared after I told them that," Herbert said recently. "I was afraid that Johnnie would come back and blind me."

Herbert suffered nightmares for months after the attack on the cousin who was a mother-figure to him. Lillie was afraid for his mental health. He would awake in cold sweats or awake screaming.

That's why Lillie became nervous when London quizzed her about what Herbert told police moments after the attack. Although three years had passed, she knew that Herbert was not strong enough to get on the witness stand and tell others what he saw.

He was deathly afraid of being in the same room with Johnnie.

Lillie was relieved when the questions about Herbert stopped. Prosecutors never mentioned him again during the trial.

Herbert never really got over the shock of seeing Wilma taken from his home with blood dripping from her eyes. When he was interviewed for this book several years ago about that fateful day, he got choked up. He didn't even want to talk about certain details.

There is no mystery about who blinded Wilma. She knew who did it from the beginning, despite being called a liar and perjurer by people who think Johnnie was innocent.

A few years ago, Wilma was walking down the street when she overheard one man say to another: "That's the lady who lied about that dude blinding her."

They owe Wilma an apology, one that she will likely never receive because her detractors have too much foolish pride to admit that they were wrong then, and that they remain wrong today.

Arrest Records

JOHNNIE LEE BROOKS

Note: This list is by no means exhaustive. I did not receive a copy of his multiple arrests for rape, sodomy and other charges. Brooks had a voluminous criminal record. Due to privacy laws, I was only able to get a list of convictions for which he received prison time. I obtained other arrests from newspaper records and court documents.

Date of Birth: October 3, 1940 (Mississippi)

1. April 8, 1959

   AGE: 18 years old

   Arrested in St. Louis

   Charges: First Degree Robbery

   Dangerous or Deadly Assault with Intent to Kill

   VERDICT: Found Guilty of all charges on May 15, 1959.

   June 12, 1959: Sentenced to 8 years in the Missouri Department of Corrections

   Released: January 28, 1965 from Missouri State Penitentiary

2. **August 14, 1966**

   AGE: 25 years old

   Arrested in St. Louis

   Charge: Theft

   Charge: Tampering with another's automobile

VERDICT: The charges were dismissed because police failed to read the Miranda warnings. It should be noted that the United States Supreme Court had decided only two months earlier the Miranda warnings were required (*Miranda v. Arizona* was handed down on June 13, 1966)

Synopsis: Johnnie, 21-year-old Aaron Clark Jr. and an unnamed juvenile were seen alighting from a 1956 Ford parked in front of a garage. The eyewitness said that the three men were stripping a 1966 Pontiac inside the garage. When police arrived, Johnnie's accomplices ran off but Johnnie was sitting the car. After capturing them, police told the men that they had the right to counsel and the right to remain silent. Johnnie refused to say anything.

Clark, however, admitted that the car belonged to him and that the auto parts is his car had just been removed from the brand new Pontiac. Since Johnnie was sitting in the passenger seat and declined to give a statement, the prosecutor said that there was insufficient evidence to arrest him without statements from his accomplices. The prosecutor also refused to arrest the other two because police failed to advise them of all of their rights under Miranda (i.e. that their statements could be used against them in court and that they were entitled to a court-appointed lawyer if they could not afford to hire one).

3. September 25, 1967

    AGE: 26 years old

    Arrested in St. Louis

    Charge: (a) First Degree Robbery

    (Dangerous or Deadly Weapon)

    VERDICT: Found Guilty on November 30, 1967.

    December 21, 1967: Sentenced to 8 years in the Missouri Department of Corrections

    Charge: (b) Failure to Display Drivers License (Misdemeanor)

    VERDICT: Guilty. Sentenced to 3 days in City Work House

    Released: December 2, 1969.

4. August 20, 1970

    AGE: 29 years old

    Arrested in St. Louis

    Charge: First Degree Robbery

    Synopsis: Brooks approached William Carpenter, a clerk at the North Side YMCA (3100 Grand Blvd), pulled out a knife and announced a robbery. Man gave Brooks his wrist watch and ten dollars. When Brooks left, the man got a gun, went to the door and fired several shots at Brooks as he got into a truck.

Police heard shooting, interviewed victim and found Brooks several blocks away. They recovered the watch and five dollars and arrested Brooks. Apparently the charges were dropped because the victim did not want to testify.

5. September 14, 1971

AGE: 30 years old.

Arrested in St. Louis

Charge: (a) Driving while Intoxicated (misdemeanor)

VERDICT: Guilty. 10 days in City Work House

Charge: (b) No State Driver's License

VERDICT: 5 Days in City Jail

Charge: Driving While Intoxicated.

VERDICT: 5 Days in City Jail

6. September 24, 1971

Age: 30 years old

Charge: Robbery

Verdict: Dismissed

7. September 29, 1971

AGE: 30 years old

Arrested in St. Louis

Charges: First degree robbery; Assault with intent to do great bodily harm; violation of Habitual Offender ACT

Verdict: Guilty

Sentence: 55 years in prison

Synopsis: The verdict was reversed on appeal, and Johnnie was tried several more times on the same charge. Convicted in third trial and given the same sentence. Brooks took appeal to US Supreme Court.

Brooks v. Wyrick, 486 F. Supp. 939, 943-44 (E.D.Mo. 1979), aff'd mem., 620 F.2d 308 (8th Cir.), cert. denied, 446 U.S. 969, 100 S. Ct. 2949, 64 L. Ed. 2d 829 (1980).

EARNEST CHARLES CRAINE

Date of Birth: May 22, 1945 (Texas)

Aliases: Charles, Louis, Scar, Scarhead

1. **May 2, 1963**
    Age: 17 years old
    Temple, Texas
    Charges: (a) Burglary (coin-operated machine)
    VERDICT: Guilty
    Charges: (b) Forgery
    VERDICT: Guilty.
    Sentence: 13 years in Texas Department of Corrections

2. **February 21, 1966**
    Age: 20 years old
    Temple, Texas
    Charge: Burglary (coin-operated machine) by Breaking and Entering
    with Intent to Commit Theft (2 counts)
    VERDICT: Guilty.

Sentence: 5 Years in Texas Department of Corrections

3. Arrest: 1972

   Age: 27 years old

   Arrested in Los Angeles

   Charge: Public intoxication or drug possession

   VERDICT: Dismissed.

4. October 25, 1973

   Age: 28 years old

   Arrested in San Francisco

   Charges: Misdemeanor burglary (coin-operated machine)

   VERDICT: Guilty

5. July 7, 1974

   St. Louis, MO

   Age: 29 years old

   Charge: First Degree Robbery

   Sentence: 12 Years in the Missouri Department of Corrections

6. May 23, 1990

   Austin, Texas

Charge: Theft (misdemeanor)

Charge: Driving While Intoxicated

VERDICT: Guilty.

Sentence: Probation (2 years)

7. Unknown date in 1992

Austin, Texas

Charge: Driving While Intoxicated

VERDICT: Guilty

Sentence: 120 days in jail on December 23, 1992

8. March 7, 1994

Austin, Texas

Charge: Unavailable

VERDICT: No Contest Plea

Sentence: Probation (one year) and restitution

9. November 9, 1998

Austin, Texas

Charge: Carrying Unlicensed Weapon

VERDICT: Guilty

Sentence: 180 days in jail on August 24, 1999

10. January 18, 2001

Austin, Texas

Charge: Possession of Marijuana

VERDICT: Guilty

Sentence: Unknown period on June 6, 2002

11. September 18, 2004

Charge: Theft of Services ($20.00) (misdemeanor)

VERDICT: Guilty

Sentence: 30 days in jail on September 23, 2004

Note: Craine resided in Texas at the time this book was published in 2011. Attempts to reach him by telephone were unsuccessful.

EARL STANLEY HARPER

Date of Birth: November 24, 1955 (Missouri)

1. Arrest Date: September 29, 1971

   Age: 16 years old

   Charge: Robbery

   VERDICT: Guilty

   Sentence: Plea bargain carrying no time

2. April 14, 1974

   Charge: Burglary (second degree)

   VERDICT: Guilty

   Sentence: 30 months imprisonment

Note: Also had a juvenile record with offenses unknown; possibly possession of marijuana.

Note: killed July 1, 1981, near the 10th anniversary of attack

JOHNNIE'S STATEMENT

From: Johnnie Lee Brooks
To: Father Ralph Wright
Date: October 28, 1971

Dear Fr. Wright:

I hope when these few lines reaches your hands they will find you in the best of health. As for me I am not at all satisfied. I sent you the diary when I told you I mailed it when you were down here. It is written on the front of a tablet, it is three pieces and a small piece. I don't know why you haven't got the letter so I am going to send you another one.

WEDNESDAY, September 22, 1971

Wednesday morning around 8 or 9 I went out to work on my car. I worked on it until around noon. Then I went to my mother's house for a while. Then I went to get my car, went to [unknown word] and Madison to the auto repair shop on the corner to see a man about a headlight bucket and tire off an old Cadillac he had sitting there. We talked about the fender I had put on my car. He said if he could get another [car] body better than his [current one] he would give me a light bucket and tire.

When I got ready to leave, my battery was down. I had left my lights on. He brought his charger out and jumped my car off. I then went to see Mr. Strain, asked him about a tire off of an old Cadillac that he had had a long time ago.

He and I talked for some time about how I had fixed the car. When I left there I just rode around to different places as I came to various auto salvage places until late that evening.

I don't know what time I met Mr. Brown but he wanted to use my car. I said okay. I let him drive. We went various places. He kept the car all that night. When we got to the tavern he went to, I went in the car and slept until he came out.

It was when the tavern closed when he came out and went to his girlfriend's house. I stayed in the car. He stayed in there quite a while before he came out. When he came out he went to his wife's house on Grand and Hebert. I stayed in the car there.

THURSDAY, September 23

When he came out to go to work he said he was late. He asked me if I was still going to take him to work. He said he worked in Springfield and I [asked him where] and then he told me Chrysler in Fenton. I didn't know the way so he drove.

We left and started going there. That's when I asked him what if I got lost on the way back? So he said why don't you get a friend to go with you?

We turned around and went to Gene Watson's house in the 3700 block of Cote Brilliante. His people said that Gene had just come in and that he was drunk and they couldn't get him up, so we left and went to Ronnie [Clower's] house on Sarah and Enright.

He was still in bed. I went in and waited until he got dressed. I talked with his mother. *We were going to put in an application out there.*

Brown told me that if I put in one he would talk to his foreman and he might be able to get me on his shift.

We were in Ronnie's house for a while so the boy [authors' note: what boy?] blew my horn. When we left there we went to the Vandeventer and Highway 40 entrance to the Clark Service Station where Brown bought two dollars worth of gas. I checked the oil and it was a quart low, so I told the man to put in a quart of the cheapest oil he had.

When he put the oil in, Brown said he was just going to pay for the gas. *I told him to pay for [the oil] and I would give [the money] back to him Friday. He said okay.*

When we got ready to leave I had to jumpstart the car because we were out of gas when we pulled into the station and didn't know it. When the car started the lights wouldn't come on, so I had to fix them. When I fixed them we went out Highway 40 to Interstate 244 with Brown explaining the way to go as we went.

When we got to the plant, Brown turned the car around and sat there for a while telling us how to get back. He said he understood why I wanted someone with me, [because] if I got lost I wouldn't be by myself. I said "That's right. If we run out of gas or have any trouble, it would two of us walking back to St. Louis instead of one."

I had around 60 or 65 cents in my pocket [note: from where?] as I got behind the wheel and we left. On our way back to I-244 I made the wrong turn into a one-way street. I had to back out.

When we got on I-244 I couldn't drive fast because the tire I put on was worse that the one that blew out . . . On the highway, the car started trying to cut out. Ronnie and I talked about that.

9:00 – 9:30 am:

We went to Kossuth and Newstead to Ronnie's house. When we left there, I thought we were going to his girlfriend's house, but when I started [to drive] to his girlfriend's house he said we were going [instead] to Kingsbury [in University City]. I didn't know where that was, but Ronnie said that he did.

I was going to stop by the house [?] first. When I went down Vandeventer at Lincoln, Earl [Harper] stopped me and asked me where I was going. I told him. I asked him why he wasn't in school, and he said that he had quit. He asked could he go with us to Kingsbury, and I said yes. We left there and went to Kingsbury.

We stayed there for a while, maybe 10 or 15 minutes, maybe longer. *I asked for a drink of water. I drank that one and another one.* I sat there with my eyes closed until Ronnie asked me about the night I had taken him to his girlfriend's house and he went in through the window. I answered his question.

He asked me did I have what you call a hotbox from [drinking] whiskey, and I said yes.

I had my eyes closed until the girl went out of the door or someone came in[note: Wilma went to use the phone at Simmons]. On our way to Ronnie's house I picked up Earl's friend [Earnest aka Scar]. He was going to his sister's house.

When we were at Ronnie's house, he [Scar] asked me if I had a knife. [note: but why would Scar ask for a knife at this point, since he hadn't seen Wilma; thus, no plan to rob her?]. I told him: "No, I don't carry a knife." So he asked Ronnie for one.

Ronnie went into the house and got one. He told me to pick him up in an hour or hour and a half and I showed him my gas hand [how little gas was indicated]. I told him that if I got hold of any gas money, *I would be back to pick him up.*

I left his house and went to Kennerly. I parked because I was just about out of gas. The boy they call Scar went through the alley to his sister's house. I don't know where Earl went. I went to Tate's around the corner. I asked him if he had any money. He said that he didn't have any right then. While I was [at Tate's], Mr. Strain came by. We talked about my car and a man that Tate had done more work for or was going to do some. He was in his truck.

He parked it on the street by the mail box. When Mr. Strain left, Sammie came by. He wanted me to fix his car. He had had a wreck and his transmission wasn't charging. We needed a snatch bar to fix his car, so we went out to Cottage Avenue in the 3900 – 3931 Cottage – to get Stan's snatch bar.

I knocked on his door seven or eight times but no one answered so we left. I told Sammie that the other person I knew who had a bar was on Broadway at Vandeventer and St. Louis Avenue. Stan went outdoors. I told Sammie to catch him.

We did on Natural Bridge at the light. I asked him for his bar. His friend had it but he said I could get it the following week. We left him, went back on Vandeventer. I backed his car into the tree, fix his bumper.

He picked up his girlfriend. I started to Cheatham's [house] and my stepson came up. He wanted some money. I didn't have any to give him. I asked him what his mother was doing. He said nothing. I told him to tell her that I would be home in a few minutes to eat. He said okay and left.

Melvin stopped me. We stood and talked for a few minutes. He was going to Mrs. Walker's to buy himself some cookies, he said. I went there with him. Then I went in my mother's house, *got a couple of lemon drops* I had on top of the cupboard in the hall. When I came out Melvin was standing on the corner waiting on me. I walked to Vandeventer and Cottage with him, told him to tell my girlfriend I would be there in a few minutes. He said okay.

I went to Cheatham's house, talked with him for a while, smoked two or three of his cigarettes and drank a cup of coffee. We went into his living room. I played with his baby son.

I asked him to take me to Dan Plackey Chevrolet to see Mr. Faris about some money he owed me. He said that he couldn't because he was baby sitting, plus his car wasn't working right. I had fixed one side of the stabilizer but the other side was missing.

When I got ready to go he offered me the last cigarette that was in the pack. If refused but he said he had some more plus he didn't like them anyway because they weren't his regular brand.

He said his doctor ordered him to slow down or stop smoking. I left his house, met Mrs. Howard's daughter. She was going down to Mrs. Peoples' house. I walked with her until I got to Jerry's house.

He and his wife were cleaning the back yard. We talked for a few minutes. I left there, went through the alley back to Tate's, stayed there kidding around for a while. Sammie came back.

I asked him to take me to Ronnie's house. He didn't have enough gas. *When I asked Tate for a cigarette, he gave me a dollar*. I went to Mrs. Walker's [store], bought a pack of cigarettes, and *asked Sammie if the change would help him*. He said yes.

We got the gas, then went to Ronnie's house. His mother said that he was gone. I told her to tell him that I came by. She asked me who I was, so I told her. We left there [why didn't Sammie testify to this?]

We left there, and went on Kossuth in the alley to the boy's house who had promised me a tire off of a beige 1960 Buick that he had sitting in the back yard, but his truck was gone so we left.

We went over to Market and Prairie. *I bought a quart of beer* with the 60 cents that I had from that morning [then why didn't he buy the cigarettes with it?]

We went on [unknown word], where I met one of Ronnie's friends, a dude called Johnnie Boy. I asked him had he saw Ronnie. [why is he so concerned about finding Ronnie?]

If I am not mistaken, he said that he had seen him earlier. When I was on Lincoln Avenue, I met a man who said that he had been by the shop several times looking for me.

He wanted me to check his car out. He had bought a '66 or '67 Buick. I adjusted his carburetor and I told him what the trouble was. He gave me his telephone number and address and two dollars and told me to call or come by his house that Friday, which was the next day. [then why didn't he say tomorrow? ; must have been Wednesday]

After I left him, I stayed on Lincoln until I went to get my car. (My brother-in-law said that I took some boy out west but I forgot what street I took him on).

That night, I went down to Ellis' Funeral Home. I didn't see Mr. Faris's car, so I started back home. When I got to Vandeventer near the 905 store, a car stopped in front of me and I had to jam my brakes. They held long enough to give the car a rolling stop.

The damage to the man's car was just a scratch. So he said he would bring it down to the shop and I could fix it.

The police said that was fine until I showed them the ticket that I had gotten for not having license plates. They said that if I took the car home, they would not give me another ticket. I said alright.

We then went to St. Ferdinand and Vandeventer to get this boy's father's car and I parked mine about three doors from my mother's house and went with him to South St. Louis to a relative's house. I stayed in the car until he came out.

When we got ready to leave, his car wouldn't start. We checked it out, then walked to several taverns trying to find someone to give us a hot shot or find someone that had jumper cables.

So as we were walking his cousin and niece came along with a friend, and the friend said he would try to push our car to start it. So he tried to push it. At one time, it started but died and so we waited until this man came back and this time the boy made this wide turn around a parked police car to make a right turn.

The police stopped him and talked with him and his cousin and niece, and then me.

They locked me up on a robbery charge because the Deer and Eastern Police Station had a warrant out for my arrest. I stayed there until [Deer and Easton] police officers came after me. I also gave the boy a dollar for gas. [From the two dollars he had?] Then they left.

The [Deer Street] detectives tried to get in touch with the man who had the robbery charge put on me but were unable to reach him that night.

FRIDAY, SEPTEMBER 24

The next morning the man came down to the station and told how everything happened but the police said I still had to go to Central lockup before I could go home. I went to Central.

I got sick and was taken to Homer G. Phillips Hospital and was checked in. But I had to check out because there wasn't anyone to guard me and the officer called Central and they said for me to check out because I was free to go.

I would have to check back in on my own, which I did around 9:00 or 9:30.

The policeman that took me back to Central said that he would check on me to see whether I made it to the hospital alright. When I got home, I drank some sugar and water, took a bath, and then my mom, girlfriend and brother went to the hospital with me.

Earl met me as I was leaving my Mom's house. He asked me what I got locked up for.

I asked him *what the police was looking for him for*. He said nothing. He said he was going to check with someone he knew, so I went on to the hospital.

When I got there, I checked with the lady at the desk. I told her I had checked in. I have bronchitis when I am smoking. I coughed a lot, so I went outside to smoke. After I was there for a while, I started feeling better.

I told my peoples that I would come back the next day after I see Mr. Faris and get my money.

I walked my mom home, got some stew and walked my girlfriend home. And there I stayed until the next day.

[end of statement]

Bibliography

COURT CASES

Trial

State of Missouri v. Johnnie Lee Brooks, Cause No. 2648-T-1971.

Barbara Drury: Deposition of December 13, 1974, Cause No. 2648-T-1971.
Ralph Wright: Deposition of December 13, 1974, Cause No. 2648-T-1971.
George Curry: Deposition of January 8, 1975, Cause No. 2648-T-1971.
"Motion for A New Trial," July 5, 1972, Cause No. 2648-T-1971.
"Motion for A New Trial," June 3, 1975, Cause No. 2648-T-1971.

Miranda v. Arizona, 384 U.S. 436 (1966)
North Carolina v. Pearce, 395 U.S. 711 (1969)

Appellate

State v. Brooks, 513 S.W. 2d 168 (1973)
State v. Brooks, 551 S.W. 2d 634 (1977)
Brooks v. State, 486 F. Supp. 939 (1979)

Brooks v. Wyrick, 486 F. Supp. 939, 943-44 (E.D.Mo. 1979), aff'd mem., 620 F.2d 308 (8th Cir.), cert. denied, 446 U.S. 969, 100 S. Ct. 2949, 64 L. Ed. 2d 829 (1980).

VIDEO RESOURCES

"See No Evil," (Columbia Pictures/Filmway Pictures, 1971)
"Longstreet," (ABC Television series, 1971-72)

MISCELLANEOUS

Jernigan, Kenneth. "Blindness: Is Literature Against Us?" National Federation for the Blind (July 3, 1974).
www.nfb-tennessee.org/jernigan/banquet74.doc

Tjaden, Patricia and Nancy Thoennes. "Prevalence, Incidence and Consequences of Violence Against Women: Findings From the National Violence Against Women Survey."
National Institute of Justice; Centers for Disease Control and Prevention. November 1998.

"Longstreet Fan's Episode Guide."
http://longstreetfan.com/episodeguide.html

Bureau of the Census. "Prices and Price Indexes". *Historical Statistics of the United States: Colonial Times to 1970. Part 1.*

United States Crime Rates 1960 – 2004.
http://www.disastercenter.com/crime/uscrime.htm

Bibliography

"The Facts on Domestic, Dating, and Sexual Violence," Family Violence Prevention Fund.
http://www.endabuse.org/content/action_center/detail/754

MAGAZINES

Dunn, Betty. "A Brave Girl Makes a Home in a World of Touch and Sound," *Life*, June 23, 1972, p. 70-71.
"To Wilma Chestnut, An Official Tribute," *Official Karate*. June 1974.

NEWSPAPERS

Abbreviations
SLGD: *St. Louis Globe-Democrat*
SLPD: *St. Louis Post-Dispatch*

1966

"Warrants Refused in Car Stripping; Circuit Attorney's Office Again Rules Evidence in Case Was Insufficient." *SLGD*, August 20, 1966.

1967

"Man Gets 8 Years on Robbery Charge." *SLGD*, December 1, 1967.

Bibliography

1970

"YMCA Clerk Robbed, Suspect Is Arrested." *SLPD*, August 20, 1970.

1971

"Man Is Charged With Blinding Girl, 17, Who Witnessed Theft." *SLGD*, October 2, 1971.

"All Money in World Can't Undo Damage" to Blinded Girl." *SLGD*, October 5, 1971.

"Offers of Help Flood in For Girl Blinded in Attack." *SLGD*, October 6, 1971.

"Crime Repeaters – A Growing Menace." *SLGD*, October 6, 1971.

"Blinded Girl Bravely Walks in Darkness." *SLGD*, October 7, 1971.

"Plight of Blinded Girl is Bringing National Response." *SLGD*, October 8, 1971.

"Hospitalized Suspects Denies Blinding Girl." *SLPD*, October 8, 1971.

"Inmate Offers Eye to Blinded Girl." *SLGD*, October 9, 1971.

"Symington Aid Asked in Fund Drive for Wilma." *SLGD*, October 11, 1971.

"Sixth Graders Collect $512 for Blinded Girl." *SLGD*, October 12, 1971.
"Blinded Girl Learning to Play Games by Touch." *SLPD*, October 13, 1971

Bibliography

"Famous and Obscure Offer to Help Wilma." *SLGD*, October 13, 1971.

"Irrepressible Wilma: She Refuses to Live in Dark World." *SLGD*, October 15, 1971.

"Man Accused of Blinding Wilma Is Denied Bond." *SLGD*, October 16, 1971.

"More Mail, Marathon Run for Wilma." *SLPD*, October 18, 1971.

"Wilma Prepares for School as Fund Nears $80,000." *SLGD*, October 19, 1971.

"Eight Young Newsboys Give $52 Earnings to Fund for Wilma." *SLGD*, October 20, 1971.

"Office Set Up to Handle Wilma's Calls." *SLGD*, October 21, 1971.

"Father of Six Collects $216 for Wilma's Fund." *SLGD*, October 23, 1971.

"Girl Speedsters Run Up Fund for Wilma Chestnut." *SLGD*, October 25, 1971.

"Volunteers Urged to Join Wilma Chestnut Drive." *SLGD*, October 26, 1971.

"Concerned Pupils Get a Letter from Nixon." *SLGD*, October 28, 1971.

"Wilma is Preparing to Leave Hospital." *SLGD*, October 30, 1971.

"Juvenile Certified for Trial as Adult in Chestnut Case." *SLPD*, November 4, 1971.

"Two Indicted in Attack on Wilma Chestnut." *SLGD*, November 4, 1971.
"Normandy Gives $256 to Chestnut Fund." *SLGD*, November 5, 1971.

"Wilma Fund Donations Top $75,000." *SLGD*, November 6, 1971.

Bibliography

"Cycle Meet Sunday Will Aid Wilma." *SLGD*, November 9, 1971.

"Wilma Chestnut Honored." *SLGD*, November 29, 1971.

"Young Blinding Victim Finds School Beautiful." *SLPD*, December 1, 1971.

"Girl Blinded in Attack Begins Rehabilitation." *New York Times*, December 5, 1971.

"Wilma's In Spirit of Season; "'I'm Doing Pretty Good," Girl Blinded in Attack Says.'" *SLGD*, December 25, 1971.

1972

"Trial May 22 For Suspect in Wilma Chestnut Blinding." *SLGD*, March 22, 1972.

"Brooks Admitted Blinding Wilma, Witness Says." *SLGD*, May 24, 1972.

"Wilma Chestnut Takes Stand to Tell of Events Leading Up to Blinding." *SLGD*, May 25, 1972.

"State Rests Brooks Case, May Go to Jury Today." *SLGD*, May 26, 1972.

"Brooks Is Found Guilty Of Blinding and Robbery." *SLGD*, May 27, 1972.

"Ex-Convict Guilty in Blinding of Girl; Cut Robbery Victim's Eyes to Prevent Identification." *New York Times*, May 28, 1972.

"2 Mothers, 2 Views on Blinding Incident." *SLPD*, May 28, 1972.
"New Door Opening in Wilma's Life; A Neat Brick House – 'Exactly What I Wanted.'"

SLGD, June 5, 1972.

"Brooks Protests Innocence at Sentencing." *SLGD*, August 5, 1972.

"Chestnut Case Inmate Slashes Throat in Jail." *SLGD*, August 16, 1972.

"Brooks Held at Penitentiary After Suicide Attempt." *SLGD*, August 17, 1972.

"Monk Here Convinced Brooks in Innocent." *SLPD*, August 18, 1972.

1973

"Brooks Still Denies Blinding Girl." *SLPD*, April 11, 1973.

"New Trial Asked for Brooks in Wilma Chestnut Blinding." *SLPD*, April 17, 1973.

"Appeal in Blinding Case." *SLPD*, October 5, 1973.

"Prosecution to be Renewed in Blinding of Wilma Chestnut." *SLPD*, December 28, 1973.

"Crusades of Two Different Kinds." *SLGD*, December 28, 1973.

"Review of Mistrial Ruling to be Sought." *SLGD*, December 29, 1973.

1974

"Key Witness in Case Against Brooks Found." *SLGD*, January 3, 1974.

Bibliography

"Wilma Has No Bitterness, But Can't Forgive." *SLGD*, January 7, 1974.

"Injustice With a Twist." *SLGD*, January 10, 1974.

"Motions Expected to be Filed Today in Brooks Ruling." *SLPD*, January 11, 1974.

"State Assails Appeals Court in Brooks Case." *SLGD*, January 12, 1974.

"Sentencing Set for Man in Blinding Case." *SLPD*, January 24, 1974.

"Supreme Court Hearing Sought in Brooks Case." *SLGD*, February 14, 1974.

"Johnnie Lee Brooks Trial Set June 17." *SLPD*, June 17, 1974.

"Alleged Accomplice Implicates Brooks in Chestnut Blinding." *SLGD*, July 2, 1974.

"Retrial Begins Into '71 Blinding of Wilma Chestnut." *SLPD*, November 16, 1974.

"New Witness Says Brooks Told of Blinding." *SLPD*, November 18, 1974.

"Another Mistrial in Brooks Case." *SLGD*, November 19, 1974.

"New Brooks Trial Starting in Chestnut Blinding Case." *SLGD*, November 30, 1974.

1975

"Johnnie Lee Brooks Goes on Trial Again." *SLPD*, April 25, 1975.

"Wilma Chestnut Takes Stand in Brooks' Trial." *SLGD*, April 25, 1975.

"Assault Charge Against Brooks to be Dropped." *SLGD*, April 26, 1975.

"Brooks Conviction May Be Appealed." *SLGD*, April 28, 1975.

"Presentence Hearing for Brooks is Postponed Until May 12." *SLGD*, May 3, 1975.

"Arguments Filed in Brooks Sentencing." *SLGD*, May 13, 1975.

"Brooks Sentencing Sect for June 2." *SLGD*, May 15, 1975.

"Brooks is Sentenced to 55 Years." *SLGD*, June 13, 1975.

1977

"Conviction Upheld in Chestnut Case." *SLGD*, February 23, 1977.

"Appeal Denied in Chestnut Case, *SLPD*, June 15, 1977.

1979

"He Hopes Hour in Prison Will Keep Youths Out for Life." *SLGD*, April 13, 1979.

Bibliography

Murder of Earl Harper

"Crime Roundup: Intruder Kills Man, Rapes Woman." *SLGD*, July 2, 1981.

"2 Men Shot to Death, 1 Fatally Stabbed." *SLPD*, July 3, 1981.

Murder of Tonya Freeman

"Law and Order; Police Are Seeking Two Men in Killing of Two in Home." *SLPD*, April 27, 1998.

"Law and Order; Man Is Charged with Two Murders." *SLPD*, April 30, 1998.

"Law and Order; Man Gets Two Life Terms in Drug-Related Slayings." *SLPD*, December 15, 1999.

Death of Johnnie Lee Brooks

"Johnnie Brooks Dies in Prison; Robber Blinded Victim in '71." *SLPD*, July 1, 1985.

"Man Accused of Blinding Girl Dies in Prison." *SLGD*, July 2, 1985.

PROFILES

NORMAN S. LONDON

"Berry Bound Over to Grand Jury; Bond Set at $75,000. *Alton Evening Telegraph*, (Alton, IL) August 28, 1959.

"At Little Rock; 2 Acquitted of Robbery." (AP) *Harrison Daily Times*, October 23, 1959.

"Stole Mr. Moke; Ex-Owner of Talking Chimp Gets Prison." (AP), *Long Beach Press-Telegram*, October 3, 1960.

"Gets Four-Year Sentence for Theft of Chimp." (AP*), Joplin News Herald* (MO.). December 1, 1960.

"Police Officers Discuss Recourse." *Daily Capital News* (Jefferson City, MO), September 21, 1968.

Yastsis, Ande. "Agents Got $1 Million in Drugs in This Area." *Alton Telegraph*, March 12, 1971.

"Jury Finds Student Guilty of Burning." *Sunday News and Tribune* (Jefferson City, MO.), (AP). May 16, 1971.

Gavzer, Bernard. "Low Pay Defense Lawyers Mooch Liberty." (AP), *The New Mexican* (Santa Fe), February 18, 1973.

FATHER RALPH WRIGHT (Biographical)

http://www.stlouisabbey.org/index.php?option=com_content&view=article&id=100&Itemid=117

Bibliography

http://www.abwilson.com/broch01.htm

http://www.monographpublishing.com/WILD....html

http://slulink.slu.edu/events/poetry/poets.html#RW

HENRY J. FREDERICKS

"Will Prosecute on 14-Year-Old Case of Murder." (AP), *Joplin News Herald*, February 2, 1960. (case tried by Fredericks and Thomas F. Eagleton)

"Killer Waives Extradition." *The Times Recorder* (Zanesville, OH), March 27, 1957 (front page).

"Drag Racer Is Indicted." (AP) *Garden City Telegram*, December 17, 1958.

"Fight Over Bullock Estate May Shed Light on Slaying." *Sunday News and Tribune*, April 12, 1959 (front page).

"Gunman Admits 2 Deaths; Denies One." (AP), *The Hutchinson News*, May 31, 1961.

BARBARA DRURY

Hanaway, Matthew. "This stinks; Seeking help with bills after sewer backup." *SLPD*, March 11, 2007.

Pokin, Steve. "Pokin Around: At the Precipice of a Pothole Misunderstanding." stlouistoday.com, April 29, 2008.

O'Connell, Patrick M. "Inmates' art sends a positive message; Mary Drury, the 'Jailhouse Angel' who has counseled prisoners, wants to highlight the role models projected by their work." *SLPD*, October 25, 2009.

Glad Tidings Evangelistic Association Incorporated (profile)
http://nccsdataweb.urban.org/orgs/profile/526068555?popup=1
EIN: 526068555
Hagerstown, Maryland

WILMA CHESTNUT (after Johnnie's death)

1990

"Blind Competitor Faces New Test in Triathlon." *SLPD*, June 3, 1990.

"Iowa Man, St. Louis Woman Win Lake St. Louis Triathlon Titles." *SLPD*, June 4, 1990.

2003

"Resilient Blind Woman Opens Courthouse Shop." *SLPD*, December 1, 2003.

2005

"Reaching Out; U. City Neighbors Lend Evacuees a Hand." *SLPD*, September 6, 2005.

INDEX

INDEX

INDEX

INDEX

INDEX

INDEX

Wyrick , Donald   134

Y

YMCA 84, 159

Z

Zulu Social Aid and Pleasure
Club   103, 149